Bruce Larson

Thirty Days to a New You

Edited by Hazel Larson

ZONDERVAN
PUBLISHING HOUSE OF THE ZONDERVAN CORPORATION
GRAND RAPIDS, MICHIGAN 49506

ABOUT THE BOOK

This book is the creation of my wife, Hazel. It was her belief that a collection of contemporary parables might provoke a contemporary experiment of faith. She selected, compiled, and edited the parables from sermons and talks and from material previously published. I am grateful to the Zondervan Publishing House and Word, Incorporated for their graciousness in permitting us to use material from *Dare to Live Now, Living on the Growing Edge, Setting Men Free* (Zondervan), and from *No Longer Strangers* and *The One and Only You* (Word, Inc.).

Bruce Larson

Unless otherwise indicated, all Scripture is taken from *The New International Version,* copyright ©1973 by The New York Bible Society International and is used by permission.

30 DAYS TO A NEW YOU
Copyright ©1974 by The Zondervan Corporation
Grand Rapids, Michigan

Library of Congress Catalog Card Number: 74-4963

CONTENTS

Part III / DOING THE WILL OF GOD

FOREWORD

This book comes out of my own years of experimenting with ways to discover God and know His will. It has been prepared with the hope that it will help many people make their own unique and significant discoveries about the nature of God and about their own potential.

This book is based on two profound convictions. First of all, I believe God is continually revealing Himself through His creation. He is doing this in the grand designs of history, but He also is revealing Himself, as in the days of old, in the ordinary, the trivial, and the commonplace.

The gospels report that Jesus spoke in parables. He simply looked around and saw the hand of His Father in everyday things. Jesus, who Himself is the greatest revelation of God, was able to communicate God's words to us through simple parables. He spoke of a coin lost, of a farmer planting a field, of a father with a wayward son, of a woman baking bread, or of a man pressing grapes into wine.

And God is still communicating with His creatures in all of the common occurrences of our days. He is trying to say something about Himself and about us and about what life is meant to be if only we can see and understand.

The second conviction underlying this book is that few of us ever begin to be the person God meant us to be. Most of us have either settled for our present state or, at most, aspire to being a little better than we are with some more self-effort or education.

But the recurring message of the New Testament is that we can be so much more than we are. In fact, it promises that our spirits can be so linked with God, by the invasion of His Holy Spirit, that we begin to see with His eyes and love with His love and be a part of His creation and recreation.

This little book, then, is based on these two convictions: that God is revealing Himself daily in the commonplace and that, in Him, you can be more than you are — in fact, you can be *new*. I feel sure that anyone who will agree to read the book with the following stipulations can discover these for himself.

This book is *not* meant to be read at one sitting. It is a series of daily experiments. Simply read one of these each day for thirty consecutive days. Read it sometime in the morning, at the beginning of each day. Then apply the lesson during that day. Explore and experiment to see whether or not this particular insight is true for you. Notes should be kept about reactions and experiences. A blank page is provided for this after each daily exercise. By keeping this journal, you will begin to discover a God who is trying to communicate something fresh and exhilarating and exciting to you as a unique creation.

If you are now in a small group or want to start a study group or house-church, perhaps each member could covenant to do the same exercises individually and then report to each other when the group meets on all that each has been involved in as a result of these daily experiments.

Whether this experiment is conducted alone or as a group, I believe God has a great adventure for each one of us, and that adventure must begin where we are. It begins as we raise our own capacity for expectation — the expectation that God will begin to meet us as we look for Him in everyday occurrences. And in this great adventure, even though He begins where we are, He will not leave us as He finds us!

Part I

DISCOVERING
THAT I AM A CHILD OF GOD

The new you must find the true you, and the true you is reflected in the eyes of your Father who loves you just as you are.

1

Parable: The Letter

It seems I never lose my childlike sense of anticipation for what the daily mail might bring. Usually
it's bills or circulars or endless printed things. But on
the good days I find a letter from an old friend or
from one of our children away at school or a letter
of appreciation from someone who is reading one of
my books.

One of those welcome letters came recently from
a minister in Grand Rapids, Michigan. We had never
met, but it seems that while he was reading my
book, *Ask Me To Dance,* his seventeen-year-old son
was killed in an automobile accident. This new
friend went on to tell me how the book had been a
needed reminder for him and his wife of God's love
and resources in this time of grief. He also enclosed
a copy of a letter he had written to his son on the
day he was born which was to have been opened on
the boy's eighteenth birthday — the birthday he
would never celebrate.

The letter tells this new little boy of his parents' feelings as they anticipated his arrival and of their excitement about his birth. It goes on to talk of their hopes and dreams for his future and ends with these two wonderful paragraphs:

There are so many things that I should like to say to you today, bits of advice and words of suggestion for the life that awaits you. Suffice it all to say that you and your wonderful mother have made me the happiest man on earth. I have literally been walking on air!

... And now, you and I will be entering into a father-son relationship! Difficult sometimes, to say the least. I, too, had a father; and I know that I was a rascal on more than one occasion — and knowing that you will be a "chip off the old block," I predict the same for you. And on the other hand, sometimes I'll be a bit overbearing and somewhat of a problem to you; but do please bear with me. I know how wonderful your mother is — she'll be a referee deluxe and ever do her best to make our home always "home, sweet home." No matter what comes in the course of the years, might this passage from the parable of the prodigal son, where the father speaks to his elder son, ever govern and guide and guard that relationship between us. "My son, you and I are always together" (Luke 15:31). "Always together" in life and death, let us be.

I was deeply touched by this father's letter written seventeen years ago, and I wish that I had had the foresight to write such a letter to each of my own three children when they were born. But, beyond that, I believe a letter like this has been written to each one of us. Before you were a thought in your father's mind or a seed in your mother's womb, God knew your name and wrote you a letter.

In part He says, "John/Jane, there is nobody else like you. Nobody with your genes. Nobody with your past or potential experience. Nobody who will have your parents, your friends, or your influences. You are the only you that I made, and I want to tell you who you are and My dream for your future."

It is tragic that so many people never read the letter God wrote to them before they were born. They are like my new friend's son whose life ended before he could read the beautiful and moving letter of his father's dreams for him.

Word for the Day: John 1:47-48
"When Jesus saw Nathanael approaching, he said of him, 'Here is a true Israelite, in whom there is nothing false.'
'How do you know me?' Nathanael asked.
Jesus answered, 'I saw you while you were still under the fig tree before Philip called you.'"

Consciousness Raiser and Application

Have you ever felt misunderstood? There is a peculiar kind of loneliness that comes from feeling that no one really understands you.

One of the great serendipities in life is to meet a special person whom you instantly feel understands you and is on your wavelength. A kind of mystical relationship is established.

That must be exactly how Nathanael felt when he met Jesus for the first time. Nathanael was a genuinely good man. People like Nathanael who are without guile are often misunderstood by their peers and sometimes subject to ridicule. But in his meeting with Jesus, Nathanael experienced that moment we all long for — the moment of being both understood and appreciated.

Some of us, on the other hand, are very different from Nathanael. In overcoming a basic shyness, fear, or self-hate, we become loud or angry or negative people. But we also need the understanding of a friend who sees beyond all of the bluster, fuss, and anger to the scared child inside who longs to be known and understood.

Well, the good news of Jesus Christ is that God is our true parent and knows exactly who we are. He does not want our hopes and dreams to be shaped by the evaluations (negative or positive) of others. He knows that underneath all the negative defense mechanisms is a person unlike any other person who lives in hope that love can become a present reality and an abiding experience.

Today believe that God has written a letter addressed to you. It is unlike the letter He has written to anyone else. Don't meet the expectations of others, whether those expectations are "good" or "bad." Going to or from school or work or in between chores at home, look for quiet times when you can listen to God. Let Him speak to you through the still small voice within or through the living parables being enacted all around you at the supermarket, gas station, or in a committee meeting. Believe that God wants to show you something of His dream for you today. Believe that you are known and loved. God's hope for you is that the unique person He created can begin to emerge and celebrate life.

Prayer
Oh Lord, create in me today an eagerness to read the letter written by You about me before I was born. Help me not to settle for the evaluations of others nor for their hopes for me nor even for my own self-evaluation. Make me eager to discover what Your hopes and dreams are for me. Help me to learn something about me that I have never known.

Journal (my reactions, insights, and results)

Parable: The Blue Ice

One of the joys of living in the Washington area is that you get to read the *Washington Post* every day. It is a newspaper full of all kinds of extraneous information. Recently an intriguing story appeared about a man who was working on his farm in Wisconsin when suddenly something dropped out of the sky into a field near him. It was blue, pockmarked, frozen, and mysterious.

Excitedly he chopped off a huge chunk, put it in his freezer, and called both the sheriff and some geologists from a nearby college to examine it. For a long time they were all stumped. Was it a meteor? Was it a piece of glacier carried by the jet stream? All they could deduce was that it was frozen hard and when it melted it smelled terrible! Finally someone solved the mystery. It turned out to be blue "potty fluid" accidentally ejected from an airplane toilet and frozen solid by the time it hit the ground.

You know, as I read that story I really identified

with that farmer. If I had had a mysterious gift drop out of heaven into my yard, I would have done just what he did — gather up as much of it as I could and preserve it in my freezer. And I suddenly realized how many things have dropped into my life and yours that are just like that. We feel compelled to preserve them or continue them because we assume they have been dropped from heaven and are therefore of value.

So many of our customs and traditions are in this category — sometimes even the life-style or vocation in which we find ourselves. A family business left by a generous father or a vocation chosen by a well-meaning mother can turn out to be smelly, frozen, and pock-marked and not God's gift for us at all. In the church we are often stuck with architecture, programs, committees, or methods that have apparently dropped on us from heaven via our great spiritual ancestors. How much we need to examine all those things we've been preserving, sort out the values and priorities in our freezers, and let some of them evaporate and disappear.

Word for the Day: Isaiah 43:18-19 (Revised Standard Version)
"Remember not the former things, nor consider the things of old. Behold, I am doing a new thing; now it springs forth, do you not perceive it?. . . "

Consciousness Raiser and Application

Think of all the things that make up your life: job, social life, commitments, community activities, family obligations.

Ask yourself these questions: Is this thing that I am involved in something I want to do? Does it give me enjoyment? Is it something that utilizes my gifts? Does it leave me exhilarated or debilitated? Is it of genuine help to other people? Do I believe in it thoroughly, and would I covet the same activity for others?

Find those things in your life that you are faithfully doing because they are inherited from members of your family or your church or society. Examine your job or the way you run your house, the courses you are taking in school, the committees on which you are now serving, your hobbies, your style of dress, your manner of talking, your way of looking at life, or God, or politics, or sex.

Today, whenever you have a free moment create some quiet spaces in your day and use them to think about your life and its components. Be aware that there may be some things at the center of your life that God would like to have you eliminate. Not necessarily because they are bad, but because they are not His best for you. Perhaps you heard God tell you to do something many years ago and you're still doing it because you are unable to hear Him saying to you today, "Enough. Stop." Remember Abraham was told to kill his son and then was given counter orders by the same God.

Are there things cluttering your life that are monotonous and dull and keeping you from fulfillment? If so, pray about them, discuss them with trusted friends, and then as an act of faith take steps to eliminate those things that are keeping you from finding the life-style God means you to have.

Prayer
Oh Lord, today give me security in the knowledge that I am loved irrevocably by You. Help me to sort through the contents in the freezer of my life that have come down to me from the past. May I save those which are of value to You in Your plan for my life and discard those good things which will simply impede what You have in mind for me.

Journal (my reactions, insights and results)

3

Parable: Mrs. K

When I was a student at Princeton Seminary, I spent weekends serving a church in a small town on the Hudson River — a church so small they couldn't afford a real preacher so they settled for me.

The vitality of that church was in the lay apostolate, the people who understood what it meant to be the people of God and who exercised this ministry. Mrs. K was one of those people.

Through all kinds of correspondence courses she had learned as much about the Bible as most preachers, and, more than that, if someone was in trouble Mrs. K heard about it and was there.

I've been away from that parish for over twenty years, but I visited Mrs. K in a nursing home recently, just before she died. There she was, in what I hope is a dying breed of nursing homes — an old converted house never meant for that purpose. I made my way up creaky stairs through bad odors and decaying people and finally found her. Still exercising her ministry to others, she had four or five friends gathered around to hear the opera on her little radio. Every Saturday afternoon she was hostess for the opera and could explain what was happening to her guests.

I said, "Hey. Mrs. K. It's your old preacher." Interrupting her party, she took me aside for a chat. Long a diabetes sufferer, she was now totally blind. When I asked how things were going, I discovered her husband had died and she was penniless and a welfare patient in the home, but she was radiant as she always had been.

"You know, Bruce," she said, "it's so wonderful here. If I don't feel like making my bed in the morning, they make it for me. All my meals are fixed for me, and if I ask them, they do my laundry. God is so good."

Remembering what a voracious reader she had always been, I had to ask, "Mrs. K, do you miss your sight?"

"Oh, yes," she said. "But you know, Bruce, I just remember all the wonderful things I've seen during my lifetime. Why, would you believe it, I went to the New York World's Fair *three* times!"

Mrs. K is gone now, but she's not gone. She is part of that great cloud of witnesses. With none of the externals of life that we think of as God's blessings, she still rejoiced and believed in Him.

That memorable visit with her reminded me of the scene from the play *The Unsinkable Molly Brown* where Molly sings "I Ain't Down Yet." And this ought to be the cry of God's people. To believe that God is with you in your present extremities. To say in your joy and sadness, "It isn't over. The last chapter isn't written. There is more, and I ain't down yet."

Word for the Day: Acts 7:54-58

> "When they heard this, they were furious and ground their teeth at him. But Stephen, filled with the Holy Spirit, looked up to heaven and saw the glory of God, and Jesus standing at the right hand of God. 'Look,' he said, 'I see heaven open and the Son of Man standing at the right hand of God.'
>
> At this they covered their ears and, yelling at the top of their voices, they all rushed at him, dragged him out of the city and began to stone him."

Consciousness Raiser and Application

What do you see when you are ringed about by enemies — enemies of old age or despair or death or failure or human enemies — all gnashing their teeth against you? Stephen saw the glory of God. Both the visible enemies and the invisible God are there. But it takes the gift of hope to see the invisible and be able to go down smiling.

Hope has little to do with facts, for there are always ample facts to cause one to be pessimistic, dour, and depressed. But there are just as many facts at hand to bring hope and expectancy, anticipation of marvelous things ahead. Nothing is hopeless — not the nation, your church, your family, or even your own life and future.

We do not greatly increase a person's ability to hope and dream simply by improving his condition. There are people who are surrounded by everything life has to give who are still cynical and sour. But the gift of hope is to be able to sort out and isolate all of the pluses in life, to build upon them, and to believe there are great days ahead.

Today ask God for the gift of hope and then apply that gift as you look around and within. Thank God for all the wonderful things that are already happening of which you are aware. This does not mean being a Pollyanna who thanks God for evil, but it means realizing that alongside the evil events perpetrated on us personally or taking place nationally there are also good and positive things that are just as indicative of the shape of the future. Look for them, believe them, and cultivate them. Begin to be a Mrs. K. Then wherever you are you will lift and encourage and bless people around you.

Prayer

Oh Lord, I am overly aware of all the slights and hurts and tragedies You have allowed to come to me at the hands of both my friends and strangers. Today make me aware instead of all the good things that have come and are coming and of all those gifts I possess. Stir in me the gift of joy and make me a giver of hope to others.

Journal (my reactions, insights and results)

4

Parable: The Rock Concert

One snowy night several years ago, through some rather unusual circumstances, I found myself at the Fillmore East Theater in New York City, then the rock music capital of the world. My seventeen-year-old son and his friend were at a concert there and had discovered they would be too late to catch the last train back to New Jersey and home. A midnight phone call summoned me from my bed and sent me into New York by car to meet them at the theater during the last performance.

The Fillmore is gone now, but for many years it was, perhaps, the center of the whole rock culture in our land and the last place you would expect to find a middle-aged clergyman and suburbanite like me. Before I located those two boys, I wandered around for two hours, from 1:00 to 3:00 A.M., surrounded by three thousand hippies from fourteen to thirty.

Now in my mind, hippies all kind of looked alike — a long-haired, raggedy bunch. But in those two hours I learned how wrong I had been. Instead, their appearance seemed to be communicating: "There is nobody else in the world like me." One of them was dressed like Kit Carson with saddle bags and buckskins; one was wearing an 1890 Polish officer's coat; one girl wore a granny outfit; and another was dressed like a vamp of the thirties. There were three thousand different, wild costumes in the place and three thousand different hair styles. Their primary message seemed to be, "Don't confuse me with anybody else. I'm me."

Now when I was a teenager, which my children assume was before the Civil War, girls all wore bobbysocks and saddle shoes, and guys had to conform and be like the "in" group. As we became middle-aged we conformed again — first to gray flannel suits and eventually to something more mod.

Even we Christians tend to have a kind of religious conformity. But the uniqueness of the Christian message is that Jesus came to liberate us from conformity. And the miracle of the Body of Christ is that we find togetherness when we affirm our uniqueness. I don't know of any other organization in the world, political, religious, social, or fraternal, that does this.

Like the kids at the Fillmore East Theater, we can affirm our uniqueness and say to the world, "I'm me, and I want you to be you!"

Word for the Day: Matthew 5:48

> "Be perfect, therefore, as your heavenly Father is perfect."

Consciousness Raiser and Application

Our word for the day has given a great many people a great deal of trouble for a great many years. If it really means for us to be perfect as God is perfect, then we would all look just like Him and just like each other. But the word perfect in the original Greek really means "the perfect you." And if we are each admonished to be "the perfect you" God meant us to be, we begin to understand that creation is a place where God delights in lavish uniqueness. Billions and billions of snowflakes fall in every storm and no two are alike, and so our human perfection consists not of being like anyone else, but of discovering our uniqueness and being that to the glory of God.

For today, try to find the things that you can do or say or even wear to express your uniqueness. Many of us wear clothes which communicate that we are like all of the other people in our particular economic, social, and age group. We tend to talk like people who belong to our church or group. Today try to find ways of dressing and expressing yourself that act out your own uniqueness.

Send a signal that you are different and that you enjoy being different. If you plan to have lunch in a restaurant, even so small an act as having some new or strange dish can declare that you are not a conformist.

30 Days to a New You   31

In the same way, be especially aware of the people around you today. They are sending out clues to their own uniqueness by what they are wearing or saying or doing. Affirm their attempt to be unlike anyone else by saying something about it and asking them what it really means. In each relationship you have today, one snowflake is meeting another. With all our myriad differences, we are one in our uniqueness. Celebrate that gift today.

Prayer
Oh Lord, it is impossible to comprehend the endless varieties of Your creation. Give me the eyes of faith to behold people I meet today as unrepeatable miracles. Increase my awareness of my own uniqueness as well as the uniqueness of every other person and help me celebrate those differences.

Journal (my reactions, insights and results)

5

Parable: Jock

I am a great dog lover, and our family has had a long succession of dogs over the years. While we were in a pastorate in Illinois, we had a beagle hound by the name of Jock. He was a miserable dog who destroyed my wife's rugs and the neighbors' shrubs and the nocturnal peace of the neighborhood. But he had one outstanding quality. He loved me deeply.

As I went to the church or the hospital or made pastoral calls, Jock used to follow my car and always arrived shortly after I did, much out of breath. When I saw him coming, I would always sternly rebuke him, but I was secretly pleased by his enthusiastic and total devotion.

Observing all this, my wife kept saying a prophetic word, as wives have a way of doing. She pointed out that if Jock wasn't chained or trained to stay at home he would surely be run over some day. Some day came. He was not only run over and killed — but by my own car. He caught up to me at a stop sign, and not knowing he was there, I ran over him.

There is certainly truth in the old song, "You Always Hurt the One You Love." But it wasn't my love for Jock that destroyed him. It was my great need for his love. It is this need for love that makes us destroy the very people for whom we care the most.

Word for the Day: Luke 15:11-13

> . . . "There was a man who had two sons. The younger one said to his father, 'Father, give me my share of the estate.' So he divided his property between them.
>
> Not long after that, the younger son got together all he had, set off for a distant country and there squandered his wealth in wild living."

Consciousness Raiser and Application

The miracle of God's love for us might be summed up in two words: sacrifice and freedom. At the heart of God's love is the sacrifice of His own Son, Jesus Christ, for us. Greater love hath no man than this. But God's love also allows us the freedom to make choices.

Our word for the day is from a parable about the nature of the love of God. A son is free to take his inheritance and squander it, not just foolishly, but harmfully. The father stands by and allows it all to happen. Indeed, he makes it possible by dividing the inheritance.

Your assignment today is to examine the primary relationships in your life — those relationships with the people you love the most. Are there some places where you are acting not out of someone else's best interests, but out of your need for them and their love? So many times we think we are acting out of love when we are really acting out of self-interest. We give advice not because the advice is needed, but because we have a need to control or be important. We do things for people we love not because they need what we're doing, but because we have a need to build ourselves into their way of life. Today, examine the visits or telephone calls you make and the letters you write. Do you reach out in communication because someone else has a need or because you have the need to be important to them?

Today ask God to give you a measure of His Spirit in your love for those nearest and dearest to you, friends or family. Try to see them through His eyes and let Him make you aware of their deepest needs. See if you can fill a need they have rather than a need you have. For twenty-four hours try to practice this kind of love in your most intimate relationships without telling anyone about it. See if you or they can tell the difference.

Prayer

Lord, You know what a self-centered and needy person I am. You know how much I parade my own unfulfilled needs and dishonest motives behind the mask of love. Today help me to be aware of the ways in which I try to manipulate those around me in the guise of love. Help me to love with the sacrifice and freedom that is Yours and that You will share with me if I ask. Help me to be an instrument for freeing those for whom I care the most.

Journal (my reactions, insights and results)

Parable: The Ashes

My father died when I was seventeen. I was in the army, and by the time I received word of his illness and traveled home, he was already dead. Perhaps because of these circumstances I had great difficulty in coming to grips with the fact of his death and carried a deep grief inside for a long time.

My father was cremated, and mother kept his ashes around for many years. Long after Hazel and I had established our home, mother married a wonderful man. In time my stepfather was able to suggest that he didn't want to live in a house with a former husband's remains, so mother gave my father's ashes to me. I was living then in Binghamton, New York, and I recall vividly the day I walked out alone in one of our beautiful state parks to a snowy hillside overlooking a lake — a place my father would have loved. I prayed and thanked God for him — who he was and what he had meant to me. Then I opened the box and threw his ashes to the wind.

Somehow in that act I "let go of my father," and the scattering of the ashes was to me sacramental and liberating. I am left with the memory of those seventeen years we shared together.

Word for the Day: 2 Timothy 1:3-7

> "I thank God, whom I serve, as my forefathers did, with a clear conscience, as night and day I constantly remember you in my prayers. Recalling your tears, I long to see you, so that I may be filled with joy. I have been reminded of your sincere faith, which first lived in your grandmother Lois and in your mother Eunice, and I am persuaded, now lives in you also. For this reason I remind you to fan into flame the gift of God, which is in you through the laying on of my hands. For God did not give us a spirit of timidity, but a spirit of power, of love and of self-discipline."

Consciousness Raiser and Application

For decades, depth psychologists have been telling us there is dynamite in our past. How you feel about your past and what you do with your past will determine to a large extent the kind of person you are today.

But beyond the psychological implications, Paul, in our word for the day, seems to be linking the past with authentic Christian living in the present. First of all, Paul claims that he served God as did his forefathers. He then reminds Timothy, his disciple and spiritual son, that the faith he has found began in his mother Eunice and his grandmother Lois. Finally he ties Timothy's heritage into an exhortation to live in power and love and self-discipline.

It seems to me there are two ways that the past can block authentic living in the present. First, I can forget the past and ignore it. I can believe that I dangle all alone in my present relationship to God. Well, this is not possible. Even if I have no spiritual inheritance from parents or grandparents, I still have spiritual ancestors who go all the way back to Pentecost when Christ's church was born. Our spiritual heritage is enriching, and we need to claim it and thank God for it.

But it is also possible to so glory in the past that we cease to live in the present. Even Paul speaks about trading his tremendous heritage for the present riches of knowing Christ, and this is a paradox. We ought to enjoy the past but not let those glorious memories block us from the riches that God would give us now.

Abraham, the father of the faithful, made that incredible geographical and spiritual journey to the Promised Land with his beloved wife Sarah and a whole retinue of family, servants, and possessions. When at the end of the journey Sarah died,

Abraham's words were the words of a man of faith, "Give me property among you for a burying place that I may bury my dead out of sight." He knew that however much he had loved Sarah and would always love her, the dead must be buried and authentic living must continue.

Today remember some of the heritage that has come to you either from physical parents or from your spiritual ancestors. Read the eleventh chapter of Hebrews and know that you are a descendant of all the men and women mentioned there. If you have a particular friend or relative who has died and for whom you continue to grieve, in faith bury that person out of sight. Let them go, grateful for their influence and their love and in the certainty that you will meet again. Move on unafraid into tomorrow.

Prayer

Lord, I am a unique being partly because of my inheritance from the past. As I remember relatives, friends, teachers, and companions of the way who are a part of my past, help me to see them as a special gift and a personal treasure. But, Lord, at the same time let me bury that which is gone. Free me to live in the now with my eyes on the future. Fill me with Your Spirit — a Spirit of power, of love, and of self-discipline. I ask this for Your sake and for Your Kingdom.

Journal (my reactions, insights and results)

Parable: Two Tuxedos

Though I am in middle years, soon to approach senior citizenry, I find I am still haunted by thirty-five-year-old dreams of inadequacy and lack of preparation. Sometimes I am caught in situations that stir up these childhood memories.

Recently I was asked by an old army buddy to come down to his town in Virginia to speak to the annual dinner for the chamber of commerce. It was not until I was introduced at the banquet by my friend that I became aware of the fact that I was the only man in the dining room not wearing a tuxedo. All my past fears of inadequacy had to be conquered before I could go on with the speech I had prepared. You might not have known it to look at me, but at that moment I had become the small boy from the Great Depression in a hand-me-down suit, and it was unnerving.

Three months later I spoke at another chamber of commerce dinner at which I suffered a somewhat different kind of trauma. An old friend in upstate New York was being honored as the retiring president, and he had asked if I would be the speaker at the event. He informed me that it was a formal affair and added that he hoped I would not pull my usual cheapskate act and wear a clerical collar. So, determined to be prepared this time, I called the local tuxedo rental in our town, gave them my appropriate measurements, and arranged to pick up my finery the morning of my flight. When I went down to pick it up, I discovered that the only tuxedos rented in the swinging new town of Columbia were "mod" affairs with belted backs and purple lapels and the shirts amply decorated with lace. It was too late to do anything about it, so I gathered it all up and headed for the airport. That night before the chamber of commerce in Binghamton, New York, where literally hundreds of people were attired in the traditional "waiter's suit," I was resplendent in my Edwardian tux and ruffles. To make matters worse, it was the first time they had ever asked a clergyman to speak. "Some way for a spiritual type to appear at a secular banquet!" I thought. And again I had to fight down all the old fears from the past about wearing the wrong thing to the party. You know, if you're equally anxious about being overdressed or underdressed, it's hard to win.

Word for the Day: Mark 10:46-52

> "Then they came to Jericho. As Jesus and his disciples, together

with a large crowd, were leaving the city, a blind man, Bartimaeus (that is, the Son of Timaeus), was sitting by the roadside begging. When he heard that it was Jesus of Nazareth, he began to shout, 'Jesus, Son of David, have mercy on me!'

Many rebuked him and told him to be quiet, but he shouted all the more, 'Son of David, have mercy on me!'

Jesus stopped and said, 'Call him.'

So they called to the blind man, 'Cheer up! On your feet! He's calling you.' Throwing his cloak aside, he jumped to his feet and came to Jesus.

'What do you want me to do for you?' Jesus asked him.

The blind man said, 'Rabbi, I want to see.'

'Go,' said Jesus, 'your faith has healed you.'

Immediately he received his sight and followed Jesus along the road."

30 Days to a New You

Consciousness Raiser and Application

I am convinced that spontaneity is one of the marks of a Christian faith. There is a lack of self-consciousness about a person of faith. There is no concern about being overdressed or underdressed, being "proper" or knowing "the right words."

In our word for the day, blind Bartimaeus knew that a great teacher was coming by who was reported to have the gift of healing. Poor Bartimaeus sat by the wayside, wanting more than anything else to see. Sensing that Jesus was passing by, he leaped up and said, "Look at me. I'm over here. Help me." Immediately people around him tried to hush him up. They were more concerned with being proper than they were with Bartimaeus's sight. But like a small child, he would not be silenced. He knew his one chance for healing was at hand, and he was willing to risk outraging his townsmen's sense of decorum. The beautiful part of the story is that Jesus responded to that spontaneous, unsophisticated cry and gave this man the gift of sight.

Faith is a childlike quality. If you offer a hungry child a meal or a thirsty child a drink, there is an immediate and spontaneous response. Offered a Good Humor bar or an ice cream cone, the child does not make a studied response, using just the right words.

So to live by faith means that you and I will grow less and less self-conscious. We will worry less about being properly dressed for each occasion. We will worry less about what "they" will say and think about us. In point of fact, "they" probably seldom think of us. Nevertheless, we're often paralyzed by fear of what they might be thinking. And we know that perfect love casts out fear.

Faith grows as we exercise it. Today, instead of living according to the rules prescribed by your social culture, try to do something spontaneous. Try to break with routine. This could mean befriending the checker at the supermarket or bringing some flowers home to your wife or mother. To be the person God meant you to be might mean breaking one or more of the shackles that your culture and your society have laid upon you. Look for ways to celebrate the new spontaneous you. Believe with Bartimaeus that Jesus has a gift to give you if you will break with convention and ask for it.

Prayer
Oh Lord, let me believe today that you have a gift for me. May my ingrown eyeballs, that always look within wondering how I'm doing and how others perceive me, not block that gift. May this be a day of spontaneous action rather than routine reaction. Let me open my eyes and see You and receive that which You would give me out of Your great love.

Journal (my reactions, insights and results)

Parable: The Watch

Many years ago I heard a story that made a deep impression on me. It concerned Henry B. Wright, a professor at Yale University and author of that classic *The Will of God and Man's Life Work*.

He was a man with a great concern for the well-being of friends, neighbors, and even strangers. Hearing that an old classmate had become an alcoholic living in the Bowery section of New York, he made a journey from New Haven one weekend to visit him. The visit seemed to accomplish nothing, however, and the return trip on the train found Wright in prayer for his friend.

During those prayers, God seemed to be giving him specific instructions: to buy a gold watch, have it inscribed, and send it to his friend. Knowing that God often spoke in strange ways, he obeyed. It seems the interest and concern expressed by that gift made such an impact on his friend that he stopped drinking immediately and returned to a useful life.

When the professor saw the effect of his gift, he decided to send the same kind of gold watch with the same inscription to another alcoholic friend. To Wright's chagrin, this man promptly sold the watch to buy liquor. It was a telling demonstration for Henry Wright and for us of the uniqueness of God's guidance.

Word for the Day: Acts 9:10-15

"In Damascus there was a disciple named Ananias. The Lord called to him in a vision, 'Ananias!'

'Yes, Lord,' he answered.

The Lord told him, 'Go to the house of Judas on Straight Street and ask for a man from Tarsus named Saul, for he is praying. In a vision he has seen a man named Ananias come and place his hands on him to restore his sight.' 'Lord,' Ananias answered, 'I have heard many reports about this man and all the harm he has done to your saints in Jerusalem. And he has come here with authority from the chief priests to arrest all who call on your name.'

But the Lord said to Ananias, 'Go! This man is my chosen instrument to carry my name before the Gentiles and their kings and before the people of Israel.'"

Consciousness Raiser and Application

The secret to spiritual effectiveness is being able to cooperate with God's Holy Spirit. This simply means being able to perceive God's will and to do it.

In our word for the day nothing could have seemed more ridiculous to Ananias than to walk up to Judas's house on Straight Street and ask to see the chief enemy of every Christian in the land. After arguing with God, Ananias had the grace to trust Him and go, and that was the beginning of the great missionary tale of all time. For Saul became the Apostle Paul, God's link with the Gentiles.

God's Kingdom will not come through frantic effort or even great zeal. You and I as believers can try to promote it by knocking on every door in our neighborhood or by buying full-page ads in the paper or time on TV. This is not necessarily bad, but it is not maximum.

God alone knows when people are ready for the help He can give. Therefore, it is imperative that you and I live our life daily in such a way that God can break into our routine and prompt us to initiate a phone call, a letter, a visit, or a conversation.

For me, there are two great blocks to living in this sensitive and effective way. In the first place, I don't really expect God to speak to me and so I allow little time for listening. Now God may give us a nudge in the middle of a frantic schedule, but it is also important to take time to be quiet during the day and allow God to give us specific guidance.

But the second problem I face is that after God has guided me in one particular situation, I then expect Him to work in that same way every time. Ananias could have made the mistake of going to Judas's house periodically for the rest of his life looking for someone else like Saul. But we can never generalize on the basis of past guidance. We must let God give us His fresh instructions for the present moment. Today, be dependent upon God and His Spirit for guidance. Take time to be quiet. Believe that some of the specific promptings you feel could be God's commands. Expect something fresh from God that will make you a partner with Him in sharing good news and bringing hope and healing in His Spirit.

Prayer

Lord, help me to believe You are more eager to guide me today than I am to receive Your guidance. Out of Your love, Lord, be patiently insistent with me until I begin to believe that You want to reveal Your will in my life. Help me to act on whatever guidance I receive in spite of my fears or my doubts. May I do this out of simple trust in You. Let me not be overly focused on results, but on Your word and on my own obedience.

Journal (my reactions, insights and results)

Parable: The Sailboat

Bermuda is one of my favorite places in the world. When some dear friends offered us their home there for a week in exchange for babysitting two Labrador retrievers, I got immediate guidance to go.

Part of the fun of Bermuda is zipping along on a motor bike on "the wrong side" of their narrow and curvy roads. One especially bright day my wife Haz and I went off on our two bikes for a day's excursion to the other end of the island.

We arrived at the old harbor in St. George's just in time to see an unusual sight. Five or six grizzled fishermen were gathered around the wharf watching a young man shove off in an old double-ender sailboat about twenty feet long. "You know where that crazy buzzard is going?" one man volunteered. "He's sailing to England." And as the little boat pulled out from the harbor, those veteran sailors only shook their heads in disbelief.

Somehow the sight of that one frail craft with its

lone crew stirred something deep inside me and, without meaning to, I found myself waving and shouting, "Bon Voyage." Surprised and obviously encouraged, the young captain waved back and continued to do so until his little boat was gone from sight.

For that young man getting there wasn't a certainty. He might not make it. But he had to start out. That's what life is all about. As Christians, whether we arrive or not isn't the issue. It's okay to fail as long as we launch out. Don't stay in the harbor.

Word for the Day: Acts 20:22-24

> "And now, compelled by the Spirit, I am going to Jerusalem, not knowing what will happen to me there. I only know that in every city the Holy Spirit warns me that prison and hardships are facing me. However, I consider my life worth nothing to me, if only I may finish the race and complete the task the Lord Jesus has given me . . . ."

Consciousness Raiser and Application

The Apostle Paul felt compelled to go to Jerusalem. He knew this was God's mandate for him and that he must comply.

It is not hard to understand the feelings of his companions. Those early Christians were aware that his life would be in danger in Jerusalem. They

30 Days to a New You

pleaded with him not to go into what seemed almost certain death.

But Paul knew that life in Christ is a life of both safety and security. God offers us the security of a home eternal in the heavens. We can be secure in the knowledge that our name is written in the Lamb's Book of Life; we are forgiven. We are loved. Nothing can ever separate us from the love of God in Jesus Christ.

But our security in God does not guarantee that we will be safe or untroubled or undamaged in this life. Paul knew there was more at stake than the length of his life or his physical safety. Paul knew he did not have to find safety nor even survive the journey. What he did know was that he must obey the guidance to launch out and to risk.

Today look for the place where you can trust Christ and begin to risk. It may mean believing that the Holy Spirit wants you to leave your present job and look for a new one. It may mean changing your major in school. It may mean risking a friendship by telling someone a vital truth about yourself. It may mean apologizing and saying you were wrong. It may mean risking your reputation on a great cause or your money in something that could fail.

But bear in mind: the important thing is not the success of the venture, but that you do what God is asking of you. You don't have to succeed, but you do have to try.

30 Days to a New You

Prayer
Oh Lord, as an act of faith this day, help me to cut the moorings and hoist the sail on some project that seems to have in it Your call for me and my life, whatever its chances for success.

Journal (my reactions, insights and results)

PART II

BECOMING A PART
OF THE FAMILY OF GOD

The new you belongs to a family not of your own choosing. Let God show you your new family and help you to find fresh ways to communicate with them.

Parable: Two Churches

It all began at a metropolitan airport where my plane was met by a young clergyman who had been assigned by his bishop to drive me to a meeting sponsored by their diocese. I had never met my chauffeur before, so as we drove along I asked him what kind of church he had. His answer was instant and electric. "I have a terrible church. I've had it for eight years, and I keep asking my bishop to move me but he never does. I can't stand it anymore."

"What's wrong with it?" I asked.

"My church is full of Archie Bunkers," he responded. "Have you ever watched 'All in the Family?'" I replied that it was my favorite TV program. "Then you'll know what I mean. I've got a blue-collar congregation full of cautious, bigoted people who equate God with the military-industrial complex." For the next half-hour my new friend delivered one of the strongest sermons against the silent majority I've ever heard.

Several months later an old friend who had taken a new church dropped in to see me. When I asked about the church, Howard immediately replied, "It's an exciting church. I can't wait to see what God is going to do with it." Describing his congregation enthusiastically he said, "It's a church full of Archie Bunkers. I've never known much about this segment of America before, but I find that there is pure gold beneath their many defense mechanisms. They really are the core of America's greatness. They have tremendous courage; they work hard; they are faithful, loyal people."

Now I don't have to be very wise and prophetic to guess which of these two churches will thrive and experience renewal and which will decline in faith and enthusiasm. What will make the difference? Basically these two congregations seem the same: filled with cautious, bigoted, reactionary people. But one pastor brings to the situation the gift of hope. He sees invisible qualities in his congregation, and with his vision of hope he will be able to call forth the real Archie Bunker, the Archie Bunker that the other pastor is unable to see.

My guess is that the second pastor will live in discouragement until his bishop finally moves him. And unless he receives the gift of hope somewhere along the way, he will always be the pastor of "a terrible church."

Word for the Day: Luke 19:1-7

"Jesus entered Jericho and was

passing through. A man was there by the name of Zacchaeus; he was a chief tax collector and was wealthy. He wanted to see who Jesus was, but being a short man he could not, because of the crowd. So he ran ahead and climbed a sycamore-fig tree to see him, since Jesus was coming that way.

When Jesus reached the spot, he looked up and said to him, 'Zacchaeus, come down immediately. I must stay at your house today.' So he came down at once and welcomed him gladly.

All the people saw this and began to mutter, 'He has gone to be the guest of a sinner.'"

Consciousness Raiser and Application

An important part of faith is the ability to see the unseen. Faith begins when we see the unseen God who reveals Himself in so many invisible yet tangible ways. But another dimension of faith is to begin to see the invisible in the life of people and groups all around us.

Everybody is partly dull, unimaginative, and reactionary. But in the same way everybody has the potential to take his heritage, background, and gifts and become an exciting, creative member of society.

Potentially, everybody is a part of the household of faith.

Zacchaeus was an unlikely candidate for discipleship when Jesus summoned him down from his tree. A hated and dishonest tax collector, he could not in his wildest imaginings have guessed that the great teacher coming to his town would be staying at his house that day.

Look for those people around you about whom society has said, "They are hopeless." Your job today is to ask God for the eyes of faith. Look at that child who is failing; that colleague who is uncreative; that member of your committee or board who is overly cautious; that person who is opposed to you politically. Be aware of their potential and call it forth by a new attitude on your part.

You may not have a chance to say or do anything specific, but by simply beginning to appreciate that person — to see what he already is in part and what can emerge as his true personhood is discovered — you can work a miracle.

Today become a liberator of those Archie Bunkers who surround you. Pick one hopeless case, a person who has been confined by you to eddys of uncreativity or reactionary conservatism, whom you've been thinking of as a person with no potential. Make that person an object of your love, your prayers, and your dreams.

Prayer
Oh Lord, even as you called Zacchaeus down from

his tree and gave him a new life, help me today by all that I say and am to call forth in someone a new liberated individual who can celebrate life and bless his brothers.

Journal (my reactions, insights and results)

11

Parable: The Tie Clasp

Some years ago a friend of mine sent me an unusual tie clasp which I wear most of the time: two tiny crossed keys. Just after receiving it, I was flying with a friend on a short flight from Pittsburgh to Dayton. The plane was nearly empty, and as we moved to the rear to take our seats, one of the stewardesses caught sight of my tie clasp and exclaimed, "You're wearing keys!"

"Yes," I said.

"They are papal keys," she added.

I had not thought of that, but wanting to encourage her interest, I replied, "Yes, they are."

"What do they mean?" she asked rather suspiciously.

"Well," I said, "I believe that every Christian holds in his hands the keys to the Kingdom of God. Jesus said that those whom we let in come in, and those whom we keep out by our words or attitudes or relationships stay out."

Instantly the stewardess's face lit up. "I believe that too," she said. "I'm an underground Catholic. My friend over here, the other 'stew,' is an underground Methodist."

You can imagine how my friend and I responded to this news. No sooner was the plane aloft and the other passengers settled than the two girls came back and the four of us had a "small group meeting" all the way to Dayton.

We soon discovered that the stewardesses, who lived in San Francisco, were looking for some lively church contacts there. We suggested some names and then went on to share with them news of vital Christians like themselves in places like Dayton and New York, as well as San Francisco.

Later in thinking over this encounter, I began to wonder what would have happened if I had been wearing a more traditional symbol, such as a cross in my lapel. Or if I had been carrying a Bible in my hand. Perhaps these might have elicited the same response, but I'm not sure.

What do we mean to say when we wear a cross or carry a Bible? Is it: "Look, I am one with you. I am your friend. Trust me; count on me"? Or is it: "See my symbol? Now you know where I stand, so you'd better watch what you say and do!"

There is a creative kind of communication that we can discover as we live out our faith in the world. Those of us who choose to wear an identifying symbol should make sure it is not something just to make us feel secure, something to hide behind.

Rather, it should be a vehicle for initiating conversations, responses, and relationships.

Word for the Day: Mark 1:16-17

> "As Jesus walked beside the Sea of Galilee, he saw Simon and his brother Andrew casting a net into the lake, for they were fishermen. 'Come, follow me,' Jesus said, 'and I will make you fishers of men.'"

Consciousness Raiser and Application

The Lord has called you to be a fisher of men, and someone has said that this is big game hunting. Apparently it is not enough for us to simply pray for people and ask God to reach them. We are more than intercessors. We are called to be those who actually go out and catch people for Jesus and His Kingdom. This is what the priesthood of believers is all about. We are those who become the means by which Jesus reaches people, gets their attention, and wins their allegiance. We are the priests who are to love and support and affirm them as well as hear their confession.

I think it is significant that the first time Jesus used the term 'fishers of men' He was speaking to fishermen, and they understood perfectly what He meant. They understood the strategy that a fisherman uses in catching fish. If he uses a hook and a line, then he needs something to attract the fish. Either he baits the hook with something they like to eat or he baits it with something that will attract their attention and which looks like something to eat. If the fisherman is using nets, then he must be careful not to scare the fish.

Jesus seems to be suggesting that fishing for men is a similar science. Our parable today indicates the need to be aware of the signs and the signals we give out to people, both by words and deeds. We need to intrigue people with the reality of God, the love that Jesus has for them, and the benefits that will result if they respond to Him.

So today your assignment is to become aware of the signals you are sending. How do other people read you, perceive you, understand you? Think of the last time you said to someone, "But that's not what I meant." Perhaps to your spouse in an argu-ment, to one of your children, to your employer or employee, or to a friend. The other person may perceive something quite different than what you meant or said. So today become aware of how you come across to the other person: your words, the things you do, the gestures you make. Try to com-municate verbally and non-verbally to people around you the fact that they are of worth, that God loves them just as they are, that life can be radically dif-ferent. Try to speak and live and dress like someone who is literally bait for Christ and His Kingdom.

Prayer
Oh Lord, at the center of Your call to all men is a love so incredible, so amazing that it is almost beyond

belief. Today, help me to speak and live and dress and act so that Your incredible love can become more credible. Help me, in fact, to become the link by which another can accept and receive You and be caught by Your love.

Journal (my reactions, insights and results)

12

Parable: The Subway

During the many years that my office was located in New York City, I had the questionable pleasure of being a subway rider. If you've ever used the New York subways, you know their walls are irresistible attractions to graffiti artists of all ages — people who draw pictures and scrawl messages: some obscene, some sad, some hostile, and some prophetic.

But the message I remember best appeared on an advertising poster depicting an austere, dignified, old gentleman recommending a particular product. Someone — perhaps a little boy writing the naughtiest thing he could think of — had sketched a balloon coming out of the man's mouth containing the words, "I like grils."

Underneath, someone had written with a felt-tipped pen, "It's girls, stupid. Not grils."

And below that, in still another handwriting style, someone else had written, "But what about us grils?"

The whimsy and insight of that third message

made me wish I could meet the author, for it reminded me of the marvelous good news of the Gospel: when we are honest with ourselves and a few others we find that all of us are really "grils" — oddballs and misfits. This is good news for the universal race of those who don't fit in: losers, odd ones, the peculiar, and the out-of-step.

Word for the Day: Luke 5:31-32

> "Jesus answered them, 'It is not the healthy who need a doctor, but the sick. I have not come to call the righteous, but sinners to repentance.'"

Consciousness Raiser and Application

The devil is known as "the father of lies," and there are two lies in particular which destroy life, fellowship, and communication like no others. One is a lie about God: that He does not exist, or if He does exist, that He does not love you, or that there is a limit to His love.

The other lie is one about yourself, and that's the lie we want to think about today. If the devil can make you lie about who and what you are to yourself and to others, he has succeeded in making you non-negotiable as a "fellow citizen(s) with the saints and members of the household of God."

To believe that I am totally unlike anyone else, so much better or so much worse, means that I dare not risk revealing myself. Inevitably this closes any possibility for relationship with others.

30 Days to a New You

Now in point of fact, all of us are "grils" and all of us think of ourselves as grils in some area. But our fear is that we are the only grils in the world. Today your assignment is to look for those things in you that make you feel like a gril. It may be some fear or habit, an ambition or hope, anything about you that makes you feel cut off from other people.

When you have found the thing that makes you feel most like a gril, prayerfully look for someone to whom you can reveal that insight before the day is over. It might be a stranger or it might be your best friend. It might be your spouse or one of your children. It might be your secretary or your employer, a salesman or a customer. But whoever it is, find a way to simply reveal something that makes you feel like a gril.

Certainly there is no guarantee of a 100 percent positive response. However, as we begin to discover that our peculiarities do not necessarily cut us off from people, we may even begin to find the Body of Christ.

The Body of Christ is made up of sinners, not the righteous. When we share our righteousness with one another, our good deeds, our record of church and Sunday school attendance, it does not seem to build relationships. When we share our fears or inadequacies, our gril-like attitudes or behavior, people can respond as one human being to another human being.

Prayer
Oh Lord, make me secure enough in the knowledge that I'm Yours, whatever I may do or be, to risk a very private and secret part of me with another human being. Help me to discover the joy today of squandering myself on another, even if I end up casting my pearls before swine, so that a depth of relationship may begin that would otherwise be impossible. Let me be a part of Your Kingdom-building process this day in one specific relationship.

Journal (my reactions, insights and results)

13

Parable: Stalemate

At a seminar I was leading on broken relationships, a woman turned up who was concerned about her marriage which she described as a "stalemate."

When pressed for an explanation she said, "My husband and I never quarrel and are never angry. We simply have no relationship. He comes home from work, has dinner, watches television, reads the paper, and then goes to bed."

"Is it like that every night?" I asked.

"Every night for years," she answered.

"Do you love him?"

"Yes," she said, tears beginning to form in her eyes, "I love him very much."

"Do you think he loves you?"

"No, I'm sure he doesn't or he wouldn't be so cold and indifferent."

"Well," I said, "he must love you or he wouldn't be coming home to this dreadfully boring routine every night. He would be out doing something a little more creative or interesting. Perhaps he's hoping that one day something will happen to rekindle the love you shared when you were first married."

"But what can I do?" the woman asked.

"What are you doing now to try to change the relationship?"

"I keep inviting him to our prayer group," she replied, "and I leave books and pamphlets around hoping he will read them."

"Is this working?"

"No," she admitted.

"Then why don't you try something much more radical and costly?"

"Give me a for instance."

I grabbed at something wild. "Some night when he is watching television, why don't you put on your prettiest nightie and your best perfume, jump into his lap and tell him that you love him as much as ever. What do you think his response would be?"

"I'd hate to guess," she giggled.

"But what is the worst thing that could happen?"

Without a moment's hesitation she replied, "He might laugh at me."

"That's true, and this is what faith is all about in the dimension of marriage. To leave tracts and pamphlets around and suggest that your husband come to your prayer group really puts you in a superior and invulnerable position. But to do something like this gives him the chance to respond lovingly or with ridicule. Can you take a risk like that?"

Apparently she decided she would do just that,

for a few days later, back at my office, I got this letter: "Dear Bruce: I did as you suggested and guess what? He didn't laugh!"

Word for the Day: Mark 8:35

> "For whoever wants to save his life will lose it, but whoever loses his life for me and for the gospel will save it."

Consciousness Raiser and Application

I don't have much hope for you or me becoming "good" people in this life. However, I believe with all my heart that you and I can be new beings.

To be radically new by the power of Christ means we can reverse the most deeply ingrained human trait: our self-justifying invulnerability. Everything in me wants to keep you from knowing where I have failed or where I hurt. Rather than admit to being wrong, I will ignore you or put you down or argue my case indefinitely.

To be a new being in Christ means we begin to share in His life. The New Testament speaks of "Christ in you the hope of glory." If He is in us, then we can begin to love with His love which means that we can risk being laughed at, locked out, killed, and even crucified as He was. Our word for the day says you must lose your life to find it. In any relationship, if we try to save our life, justify our stance, our righteousness, our innocence, we shall surely lose it. In today's parable the woman found that her marriage could change at the point where she broke the stalemate and was able to risk being vulnerable with her dearest one.

Your assignment today is to find a way of risking your life in some relationship that means a great deal to you. Instead of suggesting where the other person is wrong, tell him where you are wrong. Instead of implying that he ought to change, tell him where you ought to change. Instead of giving advice, ask for it. In other words, reveal yourself to someone else in such a costly way that he could use your words or deeds against you if he would. As an act of devotion for Christ, be defenseless in the presence of someone you love.

To love is to be vulnerable. May you in your assignment today discover that kind of love and practice it. This will be impossible apart from God's help in Jesus Christ. But being new means that we can change even our most deeply ingrained human tendency.

Prayer

Lord, may I believe You when You say, "Behold, I make all things new." Let me know that by Your indwelling Spirit I can be a new creation. I want to be new most of all in the way I love. I want to love people as You love which means to lay down my life for them. Please help me to so live love that I can be a channel of miracles and healing in relationships.

30 Days to a New You   *83*

Journal (my reactions, insights and results)

Parable: The Beds

Two dear friends recently moved to our town from Alabama when Sidney retired from his business. His wife, Louise, is a genuine southern belle who has never done a day's work in her life. Raised by maids, she had never made a bed or a cup of instant coffee, let alone clean a toilet. They are now living in a small apartment, and her new task from God is to learn to cook and keep house.

She was making great strides until one dismal morning all the difficulties and frustrations of the past months tumbled in while she was trying to make their two beds.

"Sidney Mohr," she called, "come in here. You see those beds? I am not going to make those beds. What do you think of that?"

Now Sidney is the kind of person I'd like to be — a lover — a Jesus type of guy — and so he understood immediately that the issue wasn't beds at all, and he said gently, "That's all right, dear. We'll sleep in them unmade."

"What do you mean that's all right?" demanded Louise. "You've never slept in an unmade bed in your life and neither have I, and we're not going to start tonight."

"Well," said Sid, "We'll go to a motel."

"What if we come back tomorrow and I still don't feel like making these beds?" asked Louise.

"We'll just stay in the motel until you do feel like making the beds," was Sid's reply.

And suddenly all the rebellion left Louise and she could laugh at the whole infantile struggle against God's present plan for her.

Now that's what a lover does and that's a new kind of love. A lover doesn't respond to the situation or to the agenda at the meeting. A lover says, "Hey, let's get behind that and hear the hurt."

Word for the Day: Mark 5:1-2, 6-7

> "They went across the lake to the region of the Gerasenes. When Jesus got out of the boat, a man with an evil spirit came from the tombs to meet him . . . .
>
> "When he saw Jesus from a distance, he ran and fell on his knees in front of him. He shouted at the top of his voice, 'What do you want with me, Jesus . . . .'"

Consciousness Raiser and Application

In the word for today we hear a mentally sick man

running to Jesus, saying in essence, "Leave me alone!" Jesus responds to his need and intent, not to his words.

Much of our communication with one another is a smoke screen. To say what we really feel or think is far too painful, so we talk around things or alongside of things.

The Gospel gets right to the heart of man's need. If we are to cooperate with God, we must begin to hear people with His ears and to love them with His heart. What people are actually saying has little to do with the words they are using or the issues they are raising.

Today become aware of the people around you and the unspoken things they are saying to you. Try to hear the silent screams or the secret hopes hidden behind their words.

If you have an irritable and careless waitress in the restaurant, instead of commenting on the coffee in your saucer, be aware that something in her recent or distant past has made her hostile. Try to say something to her that will let her know she is a unique child of God of infinite worth and loved by Him.

In the same way, listen to your children, your spouse, your boss, your colleagues, and your neighbors whenever you have an opportunity. Respond with your words and actions to the unspoken thing they are afraid to say and which they are hoping you will hear.

Prayer

Oh Lord, today help me to hear with Your ears the silent pleas and screams that will be hidden behind argumentative and angry words. Help me to respond to confused and aching hearts more than to belligerent and rebellious words.

Journal (my reactions, insights and results)

15

Parable: The Calendar

We probably can tell a lot about ourselves by examining the gifts we give other people. We make jokes about the husband who gave his wife two tickets to the ball game on her birthday, but often the presents we give other people are just as revealing.

I have a calendar in my office which is given to me each year by a friend. It's his business calendar, and at Christmas he sends it to all of his customers. Across the top my calendar says, "This calendar was prepared especially for (in great big print) BRUCE LARSON. And then in very small print it says, "From the E. H. Titchener Company," which is the name of my friend's firm.

This man is trying to act out in his advertising something he profoundly believes. As Christians we are to put the emphasis on the other person, not on ourselves. To be genuinely interested in someone else, to take him and his needs seriously, is more effective than the kind of witness that centers in

"Let me tell you what Jesus has done for me (or worse, through me)."

When God spoke to Samuel in the Temple, He called him by name, "Samuel." He did not say, "This is God." To be in God's presence means we hear Him speak our name. The people we witness to need to feel we know their names, who they are, and where they hurt.

Word for the Day: John 4:28-30

> "Then, leaving her water jar, the woman went back to the town and said to the people, 'Come, see a man who told me everything I ever did. Could this be the Christ?' They came out of the town and made their way toward him."

Consciousness Raiser and Application

The Samaritan woman by the well was so impressed with Jesus that she brought the whole town to see Him. She did not accomplish this by reporting the theological discussion she had had with Him. The townspeople came because of her claim that "He told me everything I ever did."

Carefully examine each conversation you have today. Try to be aware of those things you say or do not say and the effect produced in the listener or listeners. Be especially aware of those things you tend to say to give you status with the other person. With God's help try to produce just the opposite effect today. Prayerfully ask God to help you build other people up. Ask Him to create the impression in your listener or listeners that they are important and that you respect them and love them. There are no rules for this, and your strategy must change with each person you encounter. But God will give you a strategy for each person if you ask Him.

Today the mark of the fact that God lives in you will be measured by how well the people you meet think of themselves after they have been in your presence. Did they feel that you knew their name, that you loved them, and that they were important? If so, they will sense God's Presence.

Prayer
Oh Lord, help me today to put the other person's name in larger type than my own; to relate and listen and interact with another person so that he may come to know something of his own importance to You.

Journal (my reactions, insights and results)

16

Parable: Crazy Charlie

I would love to think of myself as a "St. Francis" type. He is one of my heroes, and though I don't think I have his temperament, I do emulate him every morning when I scatter seed for the birds on our back deck. (My wife has been threatening to buy me a pair of sandals and a brown bathrobe with a hood.)

The example of St. Francis prompted an incident last spring that has given me a better understanding of what it means to communicate the Gospel. One morning as I rode to work on my little motorcycle I almost ran over a big box turtle. Thinking of my hero, I stopped to move him off the road and possibly save his life. But in the midst of my good deed for the day I changed my mind and decided instead to play a trick on him. I put him in my pocket and took him to the office.

All day long that turtle was the center of attention. Beautiful secretaries, busy executives, and assorted visitors all fussed over him. He sat in air-conditioned splendor eating bacon, bread, peanut butter, lettuce, and whatever his little heart desired. The staff eats lunch together at the office, and on this particular day a friend joined us and brought her guitar. So along with everything else, the turtle heard beautiful music, great singing, and all the while continued to stuff his little belly full of exotic foods.

That night at 5:00 I took him back to the same place in the road where I had found him. I carried him to the side and headed him toward the swamp. And then it hit me! I wondered what kind of a tale he would tell his friends. How could he communicate to them the wonders of air-conditioning, the topography and geography of an office building, the experience of being surrounded by beautiful girls and eating strange foods and hearing wonderful music and singing. I'm sure that from that time forward he became known as "Crazy Charlie" to all the other turtles in the swamp.

There is no way that the authentic experience he had can ever be communicated to his friends. The more he tries, the more alienated and estranged he will become. Crazy Charlie is like so many Christians who have had a dramatic conversion or a mountain-top experience of ecstacy or spiritual heights. They try to relate that experience to people who have no equipment for understanding it, and often they simply alienate others and minimize their own credibility.

30 Days to a New You   95

Word for the Day: 1 Corinthians 14:16-17

> "If you are praising God with your spirit, how can one who finds himself among those who do not understand say "Amen" to your thanksgiving, since he does not know what you are saying? You may be giving thanks well enough, but the other man is not edified."

Consciousness Raiser and Application

To discover that there is a God who loves us, who cares about us, who forgives us, who has a place in the heavens prepared for us for all time is the most exhilarating experience any human being can possibly have.

It is sad when we let that experience alienate us from those about us. Our witness may be a well-intentioned effort at communicating to our family or friends the wonders of the daily discovery that we are loved and forgiven and belong to the family of God. But we must be aware of what this sounds like to those who have not yet discovered this truth. It sounds as though we are making ourselves equal with God and putting them down as mere humans and unspiritual. Now this is not our intention any more than it might have been Crazy Charlie's intention. Crazy Charlie simply told that which he knew to be true. But how in the world could his brother turtles believe such a story?

No one appreciated God's gift of ecstatic experiences more than Paul. He even writes that he was "in seventh heaven." But this was never the thrust of his message or his method of communication.

Today try to find ways that your own experience of God can help you to step down and identify with your brothers wherever they are. Find ways of saying to people around you, "I am just like you. I hurt. I fear. I am lonely. I doubt. I resent. I am lustful." Now don't do this unless it is true. This is not a gimmick. But the people of God are just like other people, and we can communicate at the point of our common humanity. Jesus left His privileged place in heaven and became one of us, lived with us, and identified with us. To communicate God's love today, identify with the people around you — with their hurts, their problems, their joys, and their hopes — and see what happens.

Prayer
Oh Lord, You know how excited I am about some of the things You have shown me in the recent past. But I pray today You will help me delight in someone else's discoveries, present or potential, about their world and their relationship to You.

Journal (my reactions, insights and results)

17

Parable: The Church Board

Christians used to speak of "preferring one another in love," and though the phrase has somewhat gone out of fashion, it's still a principle that might be applied to all church sessions, boards, and governing bodies if they are ever to reach what the Quakers call "a sense of the meeting."

One church session I know of has an interesting rule. If any kind of proposal is made by a member, no one can speak against that proposal until he has first of all said three good things about it. Think of the affirmation you would get in that framework. If one elder said, "I think we should tear this church down and build a new one across the street," you would have to say things like, "Well, that's an original idea; the building is certainly old and the plumbing needs improvement," before you could say, "Listen, that's the dumbest idea I've ever heard. And besides, my father built this church."

The ideas being discussed at any meeting are

always secondary to the people sitting in the meeting and their emotional needs. We can practice this in our family situation as well. If your son says he is packing up to go off to Uruguay to harvest grasshoppers, try saying something positive like, "I've always liked grasshoppers." Later you can ask, "Who's going to pay for it?" Whatever the idea, honor the person.

Word for the Day: John 3:17

> "For God did not send his Son into the world to condemn the world, but to save the world through him."

Consciousness Raiser and Application

As Christians, we believe God has come to affirm us in Jesus Christ, not to condemn us. But in our daily life we often communicate condemnation for others by stomping on their dumb, immature, impractical, or irrelevant ideas. And when we criticize their ideas, most people feel *they* are being criticized or rejected.

The application for today is simply to make the rule adopted by the church session I have mentioned a rule for your life. Whether you are at the dinner table, at a meeting, or talking with a friend, before you criticize anyone's idea say something good about it first. This is a way of affirming a person and honoring his idea. After you have said at least one good thing, you can go on to point out fallacies or disagreements.

At the end of the day, evaluate what you think happened to the people you were with as well as your own feelings in each situation. See whether this simple rule helped you to be a participant with God in calling forth gifts in another.

Prayer
Oh Lord, today help me earn the right to criticize by saying three good things about someone else's idea or conviction. Seal my lips from criticism until I have paid the price of some appreciative statements.

Journal (my reactions, insights and results)

18

Parable: The Fish

One summer we took a vacation on a quiet and beautiful Canadian lake where the fishing was reportedly excellent. (I find I'm usually fishing somewhere where the fishing was at its best the week or the season before I got there.)

There were six of us in the rustic lakeshore cottage; my wife and I, our three children, and our daughter's friend. Every morning the two boys and I would go out on the lake before breakfast and try to catch a couple of fish. Then one evening my daughter and her friend asked if they could go with me the next day instead of the boys.

I agreed, and morning found the two girls and me out on the lake in our flat-bottomed boat with its antique outboard motor. Our luck was not good. Heading back towards shore, I was sitting in the middle of the boat untangling a line. Christine was steering, and her friend Jean was sitting in the front.

"Gee, Mr. Larson," Jean said, "I'm sorry we

didn't catch a big one to impress the boys with."

No sooner were these words out of her mouth than a fifteen-inch Northern Pike jumped out of the lake, hit me on the side of the face, and fell into the boat, where it flip-flopped wildly at my feet.

As you read this, do you believe it? I've told this story to a great many people, and the skeptics invariably outnumber the believers.

That, of course, was our problem: how to make this good news believable. As we pulled into the dock, the boys were waiting for us. I held up the fish and one of the boys said, "Not bad. How did you catch him?"

You may be sure that we spent most of the morning trying to convince the boys that the fish really had jumped into the boat. As a matter of fact, I'm not sure they ever were convinced.

Word for the Day: Acts 12:12-16

> ". . . he went to the house of Mary the mother of John, also called Mark, where many people had gathered and were praying. Peter knocked at the outer entrance, and a servant girl named Rhoda came to answer the door. When she recognized Peter's voice, she was so overjoyed she ran back without opening it and exclaimed, 'Peter is at the door!'
>
> 'You're out of your mind,' they

told her. When she kept insisting that it was so, they said, 'It must be his angel.'

But Peter kept on knocking, and when they opened the door and saw him, they were astonished."

Consciousness Raiser and Application

Our word for the day reminds us that no one is totally free from the sin of unbelief. Even the apostles in the early church doubted as we do!

When Peter was thrown into prison, his fellow disciples were so worried that they decided to hold an all-night prayer meeting for his safety and release. Meanwhile, an angel of the Lord released Peter from prison and he turned up knocking at their door. When the servant girl reported that the answer to their prayers was standing outside, the disciples said she must be crazy. And when Peter was finally admitted and stood among them, they were still full of unbelief.

Even for believers it is difficult to accept the fact that God can provide all we ask and think. How much more difficult it is for those who do not yet believe to accept the reality and totality of God's love. To tell someone that God loves them unconditionally just as they are is news too good to be true. No one has ever loved them that way. Why should God?

Today you have a double assignment. First, begin to believe the great central truth that you are loved just as you are and that the daily miracles for which you pray can happen. Your prayers can affect the lives of friends, enemies, colleagues, society, and even the world. *Believe* that peace can come. *Believe* that enemies can be reconciled. Ask God for the gift of belief.

But the other assignment for today is to bear witness to your faith in such a way that news too good to be true will be believable to the people who hear. Be patient with their unbelief. Understand that no one is ever totally free from the problem of unbelief.

Prayer
Lord, the love revealed in Your life and death and resurrection and present now in Your indwelling Spirit is beyond my human capacity to believe. I can only accept this because You have given me the gift of belief. Help me today to believe that the things for which I pray are not just a possibility but a reality. Help me to expect them. And, Lord, help me also to understand those about me who find belief difficult. Help me to communicate my belief in ways that will encourage them to trust more.

Journal (my reactions, insights and results)

19

Parable: The Conductor

Squeezing into a crowded PATH train at Newark, New Jersey, one cold morning, I was shocked and astonished to hear a warm and friendly voice coming over the loudspeaker system, "Good morning! Welcome to the PATH Railroad! Get ready for a great day in Fun City."

Those who live in the metropolitan New York area or those who have visited it recently will realize how shocking it was to hear a greeting like that on a subway train.

I cannot remember all that the conductor said, but he was truly a pastor to a worried, harried, hurried bunch of commuters rushing into Manhattan. He had a friendly greeting at each stop, and as people left the train he would open his window and call out a personal word to various ones whom he had come to know during his tour of duty on that line.

When I got off, I could not resist going over and talking to him. He told me that several years before

God had brought about a real change in his life which had altered his whole life style. This man was caring for people as he daily conducted commuters into New York City. I wondered how many people had spoken to that conductor as I did, commenting on his friendly attitude and giving him the opportunity to bear witness to the source and motivation of his life style.

Word for the Day: John 2:7-11

"Jesus said to the servants, 'Fill the jars with water'; so they filled them to the brim. Then he told them, 'Now draw some out and take it to the master of the banquet.'

They did so, and the master of the banquet tasted the water that had been turned into wine. He did not realize where it had come from, though the servants who had drawn the water knew. Then he called the bridegroom aside and said, 'Everyone brings out the choice wine first and then the cheaper wine after the guests have had too much to drink; but you have saved the best till now.'

This, the first of his miraculous signs, Jesus performed in Cana of

Galilee. He thus revealed his glory, and his disciples put their faith in him."

Consciousness Raiser and Application

It's difficult to believe that the first recorded public miracle of our Lord was one that seems so frivolous. There was a wedding feast and the wine was all gone. The bridegroom would be embarrassed because he had not provided sufficiently for his guests. Sensing this, Jesus turned ordinary water into wine so that the party might go on and the bridegroom might be spared any humiliation.

There certainly doesn't seem to be anything "spiritual" in this incident. And it does seem that Jesus might have chosen a more dramatic way of revealing His power and identity. But the strange thing is that seeing this miracle, His disciples put their faith in Him.

Is it possible that Christ wants you and me to be those who bring the wine of joy and celebration to life? Are we, too, called to ease others in their embarrassment and to make life more fun? I suggest this is not a bad place to begin. This is the motive for the first recorded miracle of our Lord, and He has commanded us to love one another as He has loved us.

Your assignment today is to try to bring into some dreary situation something that will give people warmth, life, and merriment. Today try to turn the water of dullness into the wine of celebration, embarrassment into joy, for Jesus' sake.

Prayer
Lord, You have commanded me to love my brothers and sisters as You have loved me. I'm reminded anew that You were never too busy or too important to bring joy to a wedding party or to alleviate the embarrassment of a friend. Help me today to be a person who can bring joy to a routine experience and fun to a humdrum job, and may I have a spirit of graciousness that puts others at ease in each situation.

Journal (my reactions, insights and results)

Parable: The Escalator

At 5:00 on a winter Wednesday I entered New York's Port Authority bus terminal. I was hurrying home for a quick dinner and then on to conduct a mid-week service at a nearby church. The usual crowd was lined up behind the escalators that take suburban passengers to their buses. Briefcase in one hand and newspaper in the other, I got in line and began the commuter shuffle.

Just as I got to the head of the line, a hard-faced, middle-aged woman came up from the side, shoved in front of me, planted her elbow in my stomach, and stepped onto the escalator.

Now I maintain that there is nothing easy about the Christian life, and every year I see more clearly the complications of radical obedience. What should I say to such a person? I know what I would have said a few years ago — but I am no longer free to put someone like that "in her place." I know what I would like to say. I would like to be a St. Francis kind of Christian who genuinely loves birds and flowers and little children with sticky lollipops and even pushy unlovely people in bus terminals.

Being somewhere between my former condition and my ideal one, I removed the woman's elbow from my stomach and said with elaborate sarcasm, "Forgive me. I didn't mean to shove you."

Her reaction was devastating. She turned and, since she was only a step or two ahead, looked me straight in the eye. Her face seemed to fall apart — all her wrinkles changed position. "I don't understand it," she said with apology and shock. "Why are you so nice to me? I was really rude. I shouldn't have shoved in line like that."

I was at a loss for words. The woman had reacted to my counterfeit display of love as if it were real, and for the moment at least she was transformed. I began to envision this woman as a person who had been fighting all her life for a place in line. Perhaps she had come from a large family where she had been forced to fight for food and favors and affection. Possibly she had been mediocre in studies or social graces and had to fight her way in school. Even now in some office she might be fighting for promotions or benefits or a preferred place on the vacation list. Perhaps this was the first time someone with whom she was fighting for a place in line seemed to be giving it to her graciously.

At this point, I gathered my wits enough to mumble something like, "It doesn't hurt to be nice to people." Then I ran headlong for my bus.

Headed for New Jersey, I sat in bewildered embarrassment. I had seen myself clearly. "Lord," I prayed silently, "how can I preach tonight? What are You trying to teach me?"

Finally He seemed to say, "Bruce, I've been trying to tell you and all My people for centuries that life on this earth will not be changed by preaching and teaching and committees, but by people giving up their rightful place in line — every kind of line — simply because I gave up My rightful place when I came to earth to be among you. What I ask is that you who profess to believe in Me do the same."

I never step on an escalator now without looking about wistfully for someone to slam in ahead of me — but no one does. Jesus has something radically different in mind for me: He wants me to give up my rightful place in my home, office, professional circle, church, and neighborhood. If I can just remember my Lord's strategy, I may see miracles.

Word for the Day: Philippians 2:3-7

> "Do nothing out of selfish ambition or vain conceit, but in humility consider others better than yourselves. Each of you should look not only to your own interests, but also to the interests of others. Your attitude should be the same as that of Christ Jesus: Who, being in very nature God, did not consider equality with God something

to be grasped, but made himself nothing, taking the very nature of a servant, being made in human likeness."

Consciousness Raiser and Application

Jesus says, "Greater love hath no man than this that a man lay down his life for his friends." Now I suppose I have always interpreted this to mean that I should do kind and caring and necessary things for needy people. I suppose I even considered that at some point in my life I might be asked to literally die for my belief in Jesus. In imagining situations where this might occur, I had no doubt that I would be shot gladly for my Lord.

In our word for the day we discover that Jesus, being equal with God, came down from the eternal heavens and became one of us and gave Himself to the world. This is what servanthood is all about. He came among us as one of us to meet our needs. When He became an offense to us, we killed Him. And He submitted to this.

Now the difficult thing He is asking is that we do the same for others. He asks us to leave our exalted position as those who have better jobs, more knowledge, more faith, more money or more of anything that the world deems important, to come among those who have less and be at their disposal. Our word for the day means simply that we give up our rightful place in line to those who are undeserving.

To be more specific, I am suggesting that today

116

you examine the areas where people are contesting with you for a place not rightfully theirs: in your office, factory, school, home, or neighborhood. This is where you can exhibit true Christian faith and give up your rightful place. If you do this simply to avoid conflict, it doesn't count! But if, from a position of strength, you choose not to fight for your rights, for Jesus' sake, you are doing the very thing He commanded us to do.

So today look for the places where undeserving people are trying to put you down: on escalators, in subways and buses, in committees, on office staffs, and in schools. To give them the place which is rightfully yours is a silent but powerful witness to the fact that this is how you have been loved. It may change the other person or it may not. That is not important. The important thing is that this is our Lord's strategy, and we belong to Him.

Prayer
Lord, help me today to know that You gave up Your rightful place in heaven to come and live with me in my world. Help me to give up my rightful place to other people as freely as You gave up Your place for me.

Journal (my reactions, insights and results)

Parable: The Grits

When I joined the infantry during World War II, it was the beginning of many new learning experiences for me. As a seventeen-year-old kid from Chicago, I was sent first of all to Fort Benning, Georgia, for training. My first morning I sat down to breakfast with ten other men at a family-style table. In the center of that table was a large bowl of something that looked like Cream of Wheat. As I scooped up a large amount in my bowl and poured on milk and sugar, I noticed a tall mountain boy across the table staring at me bug-eyed. "Is that the way you eat grits?" he asked.

Now as a Chicago boy I had heard of grits but had never seen them before, and I mentally filed this new information away for future reference. But rather than exhibit my ignorance, I smiled confidently and said, "Oh, yes. This is how we eat grits in Chicago." He watched me in amazement as I finished the terrible tasting concoction. And by keeping my eye on him I discovered that the proper way to eat grits is with butter and salt.

Many mornings later I found myself sitting at the breakfast table with this same rangy mountaineer. Grits were served again, and under his watchful eye I took a bowl, scooped up some grits, and poured on milk and sugar. Somehow I managed to eat the mess. The alternative, which would be to admit my ignorance or error, was unthinkable.

Word for the Day: John 5:2-7

> "Now there is in Jerusalem near the Sheep Gate a pool, which in Aramaic is called Bethesda and which is surrounded by five covered colonnades. Here a great number of disabled people used to lie — the blind, the lame, the paralyzed. One who was there had been an invalid for thirty-eight years. When Jesus saw him lying there and learned that he had been in this condition for a long time, he asked him, 'Do you want to get well?'
>
> "'Sir,' the invalid replied, 'I have no one to help me into the pool when the water is stirred. While I am trying to get in, someone else goes down ahead of me.'"

Consciousness Raiser and Application

Someone once said that the Gospel is all too often the answer to an unasked question. Certainly the central message of the Gospel is that God offers love, forgiveness, and healing to all those who admit they are in trouble.

But as the story of the grits would indicate, I have great difficulty in admitting I am in trouble or wrong. I'm very much like the man by the pool of Bethesda. He had been ill for thirty-eight years and lay by the pool hoping for a healing. When Jesus came by and asked him if he wanted to be healed, his first response was to blame someone else for his condition. He complained that he had no one to help him into the pool at the right time.

Today your assignment is to learn how to ask for help. Now to ask for help from either God or man is humbling. But I would suggest that if we cannot ask for help from our fellowmen, we probably cannot ask for help from God. The problem lies in our unwillingness to confess our need.

Today open yourself to all that God may want to give you, through His own mysterious transcendence or through the mediation of some other person (believer or otherwise). Practice asking for help. Try to find ways of saying genuinely, "I don't know, please tell me," or "How do you do that?" or "Would you show me . . ?"

As difficult as it is to admit our inadequacies, it is even more difficult to admit we have been wrong. Today may God show you those areas where you have been wrong and enable you to say, "Please forgive me."

But whether our need is for forgiveness or for specific help in some area, it is a beautiful thing to be in the place where we are open to receive from God or from any of His servants.

Prayer
Lord, today make me aware of the number of ways in which You might want to burst into my life through people or through Your own Holy Spirit. Help me to discover my own limitedness and finiteness, my insensitivity and stupidity. Make me someone who can delight in receiving that You might be glorified.

Journal (my reactions, insights and results)

Parable: The Ticket Seller

The Celebration of Evangelism held in Cincinnati was called "A Revolution of Love," and that's just what it turned out to be. It was a unique climate where young and old, black and white, liberal and conservative began to listen to one another, to understand one another, and to love one another.

When we left the celebration on Friday afternoon, I was sure the spirit of love and brotherhood I had found there would last forever. It lasted till I got to the airport and found my flight to Baltimore was overbooked and my confirmed ticket would not be honored. Eight of us who had been at the celebration watched in amazement as the plane took off leaving us behind. Even worse, the airline personnel didn't seem to care.

As we began to voice our anger, it suddenly hit us. If our faith in Jesus Christ which we had been celebrating that week was real, it had to be lived out right there.

With my sense of peace and joy somewhat restored, I began to move to the other airline counters. At one of them I found a young man who immediately said, "Let me see what I can do for you." Getting out his big book, he began figuring and typing on his teletype. "There is a chance you might get on a plane leaving right now for Pittsburgh," he explained, "with a possible connection to Baltimore." I grabbed the ticket he wrote for me and ran to the gate, only to find that plane was also filled!

Crestfallen, I returned to my "chaplain" behind the ticket counter and told him my story. "Don't worry," he reassured me. "We'll find some way to get you there." And he began to check his book again.

Just then a "celebration friend" came up, and I poured out my troubles. "Don," I said, "my faith was being sorely tested by the indifference of that airline down the way, but then I met this man here. He and his company aren't even responsible for my problem, but he's trying to help and has spent all kinds of time on me. Just to know there is someone who cares makes all the difference.

As the two of us talked, the ticket agent looked up and, without saying a word, reached into his inside coat pocket and pulled out a picture of Jesus. Smiling, he held it before us for a moment and then silently put it back again and returned to the teletype and the business of reservations. Speechless for a moment, Don finally said, "Hey, he's one of us, isn't he?" At that point our new friend smiled and handed me my ticket for confirmed space on a later flight. "Good luck and God bless," he said.

Now a five-hour delay in getting home is no fun, but meeting that unknown disciple behind the ticket counter made it all worthwhile.

Word for the Day: Acts 16:14-15

> "One of those listening was a woman named Lydia, a dealer in purple cloth from the city of Thyatira, who was a worshiper of God. The Lord opened her heart to respond to Paul's message. When she and the members of her household were baptized, she invited us to her home. 'If you consider me a believer in the Lord,' she said, 'come and stay at my house.' And she persuaded us."

Consciousness Raiser and Application

For many of us it is difficult to think of the marketplace as a holy place. We expect to have God touch us and bless us and comfort us in those accustomed institutions we identify with worship or religion or spirituality.

What we forget is that the marketplace is where God's people live most of their lives. After they leave the places of worship, the only place to serve God and their fellow-man is in the marketplace. Elton Trueblood tells a wonderful story about a stranger who came to a Quaker meeting. He was unaccustomed to the silence and embarrassed by it. Finally he turned to someone nearby and said, "When does the service begin?" The man leaned over and replied in a whisper, "The service begins when the worship ends!"

Today you have two assignments. As you head for the marketplace (be it a school, office, factory, or hospital), look for someone along the way to whom you can be a Lydia. Look for someone who needs comfort, money, encouragement, a room for the night, help with some task, or perhaps just a hand with a suitcase or some bundles. As a part of your love for God and therefore for His people, try to be an answer in a specific way to someone else in their need.

The second part of your assignment is to look for someone like Lydia when life becomes oppressive, difficult, confusing, or frightening. Don't retreat into yourself or rush for some familiar place of prayer. Expect God to break into your life through a Lydia — God's person there in the marketplace. Expect someone to say, "May I help you?" Let God surprise you with the unlikely people He might spread about your life today to remind you that you are a part of the family and that you are loved and cared for.

Prayer

Lord, today let me be a Lydia in the marketplace. Let me be someone who can look for another in trouble and offer relevant, specific help. Let me also believe that I am surrounded by Lydias in all kinds of unexpected places. Allow me to receive help from one of Your Lydias this day and give You the praise and the thanks.

Journal (my reactions, insights and results)

Parable: The Honda

After twelve years of life as a commuter from a town in New Jersey to New York City, it was a pleasant change to move to Columbia, Maryland, where much of the pastoral countryside of the last century remains unchanged. There are no subways yet! I still miss New York in many ways, but life in Columbia has made it possible to realize one of the dreams of my life — to own a motorcycle.

My fifteen-year-old son was as thrilled about this prospect as I was, and together we shopped around for the right machine. We finally settled on the smallest full-size motorcycle that Honda makes, a Trail 90. This meant my son could use the motorcycle to ride in the woods around our house, and certainly it would be the most economical and adventurous way for me to travel the five miles to and from the office.

Well, it's no small matter getting a motorcycle licensed and registered, not to mention passing the road test. But the great day finally came, and I was ready for my maiden run to the office. Wearing my best business suit and tie and with my briefcase strapped on behind, I ventured forth.

Since about one-fourth mile of the journey entailed traveling on a four-lane super highway, I picked a late morning hour so that I would not get into any heavy traffic. All went well, and by the time I reached the highway I was moving along at a speedy thirty-five miles per hour. Suddenly, coming at me in the opposite direction at about seventy miles per hour was what cyclists refer to as the "ultimate machine." It was a huge Honda 750 carrying a burly young cyclist with his chick hanging on behind, both in black leather jackets, long hair flying out from under each helmet.

As we were about to pass each other, the driver raised his left arm in the "ride on" salute that motorcyclists give. I cautiously looked around to see who was following me and discovered that mine was the only vehicle on the road. Obviously he meant me. I had been accepted into that great fellowship of "easy riders" my first time out! Timidly I gave him back a salute as he whisked by. I could not believe that getting into this mysterious fraternity would be so easy. Simply by spending several hundred dollars for a tiny machine, with no credentials, no experience, and not even the proper uniform, I was one of them — no questions asked!

I rode home from the office that night looking for cyclists. I spotted one a great way off, and before he could even see me clearly, I greeted him with a "ride on" sign which he loyally returned. Since then whenever I ride I find our special fellowship quick to greet one another.

Now to understand what this means to me you have to understand one of the basic anxieties of my life. I have a deep-seated fear of being the odd man out. The one who doesn't fit. The one who is inappropriate for the occasion. I have recurring nightmares of being at a party without my trousers or in the pulpit without a single note or taking an exam for which I have not studied. If the Gospel is to be good news for people like me it has to say, "Welcome. You're one of us. You're home free. Come on in; you belong."

Because of my little motorcycle this is exactly what happened and keeps happening. An exciting group of people have found me acceptable and have included me. And this is exactly the kind of message the church must communicate to the world and to the non-Christian. When someone comes into our worship service, we must somehow non-verbally say to them, "Welcome. You're home. You belong. We're with you."

Word for the Day: John 8:10-11

> "Jesus straightened up and asked her, 'Woman, where are they? Has no one condemned you?' 'No one, sir,' she said. 'Then neither do I condemn you,' Jesus

declared. 'Go now and leave your
life of sin.'"

Consciousness Raiser and Application
One of the sad things about life on this globe is
that so many people are trying to put other people
down. Some of my most painful memories come
from my own childhood experiences or from watching children minimize, humiliate, and shame one
another. Anyone who is different, deformed, unlovely, or awkward has no shortage of people to
point that out to him.

As we get older it seems we are still quick to point
out one another's failings. We may not be as overtly
cruel, but we are quick to make those around us feel
stupid or inferior. Life is so full of situations that
bring out the worst in us. When it rains we say, "Why
didn't you close the car windows?" When we are
behind in our bills we say, "Didn't you mail those
letters?" When we're presented with a low report
card we say, "Didn't you promise me you would
work harder this semester?" When our secretary
misspells a word we say, "Don't you have a dictio-
nary?" When our child spills a glass of milk we say,
"Do you have to be so clumsy?" The list goes on
and on as we are put down or put others down daily
for real or imagined shortcomings.

I am convinced that Jesus came to reverse this
process. When the woman taken in adultery was
brought before Him, there was a whole circle of
fellow human beings condemning and criticizing,

ready to stone her to death — which was, in those days, within their legal rights. Now there was no question about her guilt or the legal punishment of that time. However, our Lord changed the whole emphasis when He said, "Let the innocent one, that is the one who has no error in his life, cast the first stone." When the crowd left, He said to her, "Neither do I condemn you."

Today look for as many ways as possible to say in twentieth century language — to the people at your breakfast table, in your office, in your school, or in your neighborhood — "I believe in you. I do not condemn you. What you did is okay. I understand."

Each time you feel anger rising at someone who has failed you or has hurt another, try to reverse the feeling and say an affirming word to that person about your belief in them. Convey the fact that your acceptance of them does not depend on their performance. Mistakes or failures can be corrected, and it's going to be O.K.

Prayer
Oh Lord, help me to know that the heart of the good news is the fact that we are no longer strangers, but belong to You and to Your Kingdom and to one another. Help me in some tangible way to communicate to another traveler on the road of life that I recognize him as belonging to You and that he is thereby my brother and companion.

Journal (my reactions, insights and results)

PART III

DOING THE WILL OF GOD

God is not only your father or the head of your new family; He also is engaged in radically changing the world and the way men live together in it. The new you needs to be aware of the romance of doing the will of God.

Parable: The Broken Door

When the beds at our house are full and we have to put guests up at our local motel, they never fail to be impressed with it. It's so posh there are even phones in the bathrooms. One evening recently I went there to pick up some friends for a dinner date at our house. As I came into the lobby I felt something sharp on the door, and when I picked up the house phone to announce my arrival I realized blood was running off my thumb, down my arm, and splashing on the counter. Something on the door had removed a whole chunk of skin.

I quickly hung up and rushed over to the reception desk. "Can you girls help me?" I asked. "I've cut my thumb on your door, and I'm bleeding all over your lobby." In no time those two lovely girls produced Kleenex and Band-Aids and had me all fixed up. I was greatly impressed with their speed and efficiency and said so. "Well, actually," said one girl, "you're the third person today to cut his hand on that same door."

I've been wondering since then if that's what happens in my life. Have I gotten so adept at putting on Band-Aids that I never think about how I could prevent the hurts?

Word for the Day: Leviticus 25:9-10, (New English Bible)

". . . and so you shall hallow the fiftieth year and proclaim liberation in the land for all its inhabitants. You shall make this your year of jubilee."

Consciousness Raiser and Application

Most of us enjoy helping other people. It is satisfying to be able to give money or counsel or some particular service to someone else.

The Bible is clear in stating that God does command us always to give the cup of cold water, to share our coat with another, to visit those who are sick or imprisoned. But our word for the day suggests that God also is concerned with the cause of injustice or oppression or evil. The old Jews celebrated the Year of Jubilee, a year in which all debts were canceled, slaves were set free, and land was returned to original owners. As a result of this practice, every fifty years the system was radically altered and a new beginning was made possible.

Today look for the place in your family, your job, your school, or your neighborhood where you can begin to change a destructive pattern. Begin to be aware of those things that hurt and oppress the people around you and try to find the place where you can make a difference. Often people who try to change systems are misunderstood, and we must be prepared for that. But this is our call, and it is as definite as our call to individual charity and good works. We are called to bring about that Year of Jubilee to those who are being exploited, oppressed, dehumanized, or ignored. Today, look for the place where your influence can make a difference.

Prayer
Oh Lord, You know how much I enjoy putting Band-Aids on people's bloody wounds, but today help me to find that which is hurting many and to quietly repair some procedure, rule, law, or way of doing business that will keep people from being hurt.

Journal (my reactions, insights and results)

Parable: The Cab Driver

It was a beautiful fall day in Indianapolis when I stepped off the plane and climbed into a taxi. As we were driving along, I remarked to the driver, "It's really a gorgeous day out here in Indiana."

"You should have been here yesterday," was his response. "It was terrible."

We drove a bit further and I said, "You know, most of our autumn leaves are gone in Maryland, but your trees are still beautiful. I'm glad I came this week."

"These leaves will be gone in three or four days," he predicted.

We came alongside the Indianapolis Speedway where the great car-racing event occurs every Memorial Day.

"Isn't this the Indianapolis Speedway?" I asked.

"Yes," he replied.

"I'd sure like to see the race here some Memorial Day," I said.

"I wouldn't go near it," responded the cabby. "I'd rather watch the horses run."

"Ah, you go to the track?"

"No, I never go. It's too expensive."

When we parted, I was struck by the hopelessness of this man's outlook. Even the good days are bad because they will soon change. My cab driver's motto seemed to be, "Behind every silver lining there is a dark cloud."

By way of contrast, a friend recently sent me a postcard (apropos of nothing) with the following message in his great bold scrawl: "Thought for the day. If you plan to swallow a frog, it is best not to look at it too long. If you have a number of frogs to swallow, swallow the big one first." Signed, "George." The sender is George McCausland, known all over the Pittsburgh area as "Uncle George." He is in demand as a conference speaker, counselor, and encourager of the discouraged.

For "Uncle George" every day is an adventure, and for those who have the privilege of being his friends, that adventure is contagious. You never know when a visit or a phone call or a postcard like the one I received will burst into your day and lift your sights.

Word for the Day: Acts 27:20-22; 33-36

> "When neither sun nor stars appeared for many days and the storm continued raging, we finally gave up all hope of being saved.

After the men had gone a long time without food, Paul stood up before them and said: 'Men, you should have taken my advice not to sail from Crete; then you would have spared yourselves this damage and loss. But now I urge you to keep up your courage, because not one of you will be lost; only the ship will be destroyed . . . .

"Just before dawn Paul urged them all to eat. 'For the last fourteen days,' he said, 'you have been in constant suspense and have gone without food — you haven't eaten anything. Now I urge you to take some food. You need it to survive. Not one of you will lose a single hair from his head.' After he said this, he took some bread and gave thanks to God in front of them all. Then he broke it and began to eat. They were all encouraged and ate some food themselves."

Consciousness Raiser and Application

The storm had lasted fourteen days. All of the professional sailors were terrified as were the passengers. They had thrown the cargo and much of the rigging overboard. They had even tied ropes around the ship to hold it together in the storm.

People were so terrified that for fourteen days they had neglected eating.

In the midst of all this, a word of assurance came from one little landlubber. He told the professionals on board not to worry — God had told him that not a single person would die. He then urged them to eat, broke bread, gave thanks, sat down, and initiated a picnic in the midst of the storm. Encouraged, they all joined him.

Hope is contagious! Hope is the thing that sustains one person through an ordeal of unbelievable hardship, a prison camp or death march, while others perish.

Hope is a gift of God. You cannot generate hope by self-effort any more than you can generate faith or love. It is God's to give and ours to receive if we want it.

Perhaps the most remarkable quality of hope is its contagiousness. Jesus spoke about His followers being leaven or salt. Our word for the day demonstrates that one person with hope can change the attitude on a sinking ship. One person with hope can change an office. One person with hope can make a classroom more bearable or more fun.

Today, ask for the gift of hope and then begin to exercise it wherever you are sent. It may be that in the midst of some tense meeting you'll be able to simply say, like Paul, "Let's take a break and have something to eat." Receive the gift of hope today and share it with your family, friends, and colleagues in a specific way.

Prayer

Lord, I know that You live in me when people around me are encouraged; when they can take themselves and their problems less seriously because I am there. Help me to find ways today to celebrate life in every encounter, even those over the telephone or by letter. May I become a contagious person sharing hope with others for Your sake.

Journal (my reactions, insights and results)

Parable: E=MC²

When I was a student at Princeton Theological Seminary, I had a very distinguished neighbor. Albert Einstein was at that time teaching at the Institute for Advanced Studies and lived next door to the seminary.

One Sunday when I was returning from church, I saw him out walking. He was wearing his usual sweatshirt and sneakers. His long white hair was flying in the breeze (he was the original hippy), and he carried the Sunday paper. This is my chance, I thought. I rushed up to him and said, "Good morning, Dr. Einstein." He said, "Good morning." Then for three blocks we walked side by side and I couldn't think of a thing to say.

I guess Albert Einstein will always be one of my heroes. I've been told that back in 1904 when scientists were propounding the law of the conservation of matter (matter can't be destroyed, they said, it just changes form), Einstein, who could hardly pass a course in science or math in his early school years, said, "I don't believe that." And, of course, his research finally led to the splitting of the atom where it was discovered that the weight of the two halves was less than the total. Something called energy was released. Out of that came the famous $E=MC^2$ formula that has ushered us into a new age. All because one man believed that the best ideas hadn't been thought of yet.

Well, I believe that God's best ideas about how life can be lived on this tiny spaceship Earth have not yet been discovered. When I was a boy, Tinker Toys were popular, and I was thrilled to receive a box of them one Christmas. The picture on my little $1.98 box showed all kinds of fantastic things that could be built. But my box didn't have enough spools and spindles to produce the wonderful ferris wheel in the picture. I finally realized that I needed box X-23 for $14.00 complete with a motor to make the things I wanted. I was trapped in a limited system — only able to build the few things I had sufficient pieces for.

Do you believe you have all the pieces of God's thinking right now and simply have to figure out a way to make those pieces work? I believe God is aching to give us new insights into what it means to be the incarnation of His love and the tools to implement those insights so that we won't have inadequate spiritual Tinker Toys. I believe that the best ways are still in the mind of God. He is waiting for people who do not think in terms of a closed system

— people like Albert Einstein. And, potentially, you and me!

Word for the Day: Revelation 21:1-4

"Then I saw a new heaven and a new earth, for the first heaven and the first earth had passed away, and there was no longer any sea. I saw the Holy City, the new Jerusalem, coming down out of heaven from God, prepared as a bride beautifully dressed for her husband. And I heard a loud voice from the throne saying, 'Now the dwelling of God is with men, and he will live with them. They will be his people, and God himself will be with them and be their God. He will wipe every tear from their eyes. There will be no more death or mourning or crying or pain, for the old order of things has passed away.'"

Consciousness Raiser and Application

In the Book of Revelation, John was able to visualize that which was invisible and to claim it as a coming reality. He knew that because Jesus Christ came to live among us, things could not and should not be the same. He saw the implications for life on this earth and beyond.

Today, look at life about you in your particular

world: your home, school, neighborhood, or business. Believe that the best way of doing your particular job and of living life in your particular setting has not yet been found. Believe that God is eager to have someone like you discover a new dimension of His liberating, creative will for men in that situation.

You might simply come up with a way to make the job easier or more fun. You might be able to change unjust laws or rules that oppress or dehumanize other people. Believe that God is a creator who is even more eager to give us new blueprints, new guidelines, new methods, and new ways, than we are to ask. Today let God show you your piece of the world through new eyes. Begin to initiate changes, however small, that can make life new and different for those around you.

Prayer

Lord, You are not only the Redeemer of the world, but You are the Creator and the Recreator of the universe. Help me today to see the world through Your eyes. Help me to participate with You in the exciting work of recreation that will bring liberty and joy to many about me.

30 Days to a New You

Journal (my reactions, insights and results)

Parable: English Leather

Early one morning I had to catch a plane from Newark, New Jersey, to Syracuse, New York, having returned late the previous night from leading one conference and on my way to another.

I was tired. I had not budgeted my time wisely, and I was totally unprepared for the intense schedule before me. After rising early and hastily eating breakfast, I drove to the airport in a mood that was anything but positive. By the time the plane took off, I felt so sorry for myself, and so guilty because I was unprepared, that I hated God and myself and the people who had invited me to come to lead this conference.

Sitting on the plane with an open notebook in my lap, I prayed, "Oh, God, help me. Let me get something down here that will be useful to Your people in Syracuse." About halfway through the brief flight, a stewardess came down the aisle passing out coffee. The passengers were all men, and as the stewardess approached my seat I heard her exclaim, "Hey! Someone is wearing English Leather After Shave Lotion. I can't resist a man who uses English Leather. Who is it?"

Eagerly I waved my hand and announced, "It's me!"

The stewardess immediately came over and sniffed my cheek while I sat basking in this sudden attention. All through the remainder of the flight we maintained a cheerful banter each time she passed my seat. Twenty-five minutes later when the plane prepared to land, I realized that my temporary insanity had vanished. Despite the fact that I had failed in every way — in budgeting my time, in preparation, and in attitude — everything had changed. I was freshly aware that I loved God and that He loved me.

What is more, I loved myself and the people around me and the people who were waiting in Syracuse. I was like the Gerasene demoniac after Jesus had touched him — clothed, in my right mind, and seated at the feet of Jesus. I looked down at the notebook in my lap and found a page full of ideas that could prove useful through the weekend.

"God," I mused, "how did this happen?" It was then I realized that someone had entered my life and turned a key. It was just a small key, turned by an unlikely person. But that simple act of affirmation, that undeserved and unexpected attention, had transformed me from someone in a deep depression into a sane, mature Christian.

Word for the Day: Matthew 14:25-31

> "During the fourth watch of the night Jesus went out to them, walking on the lake. When the disciples saw him walking on the lake, they were terrified. 'It's a ghost,' they said, and cried out in fear. But Jesus immediately said to them: 'Take courage! It is I. Don't be afraid.'
>
> 'Lord, if it's you,' Peter replied, 'tell me to come to you on the water.'
>
> 'Come,' he said.
>
> Then Peter got down out of the boat and walked on the water to Jesus. But when he saw the wind, he was afraid and, beginning to sink, cried out, 'Lord, save me!'
>
> Immediately, Jesus reached out his hand and caught him. 'You of little faith,' he said, 'why did you doubt?' "

Consciousness Raiser and Application

Peter was the disciple to whom Jesus said, "You are Peter (rock), and on you I will build My church." Jesus was depending on Peter to establish His Kingdom after His death and resurrection. And yet He also said to Peter, "You of little faith." Well, every believer is at best a man of little faith. But the Bible tells us that a faith the size of a grain of mustard seed will move mountains.

Today your assignment is to look for people who are already believers, fellow apostles and fellow priests in the Kingdom of our Lord, and yet who are those of little faith. Many of those same people, because they have taken their discipleship seriously, have attempted some great task or have launched out on some new adventure but have begun to sink. They have temporarily forgotten that a little bit of faith is sufficient. In a state of fear and spiritual myopia, they have forgotten that Jesus Christ said He was adequate for all situations. Today, look for a sinking brother or sister who is caught up in introspection, self-doubt, fear, or any one of a thousand forms of unbelief.

Try to find a way to give that person the word of affirmation or encouragement that will trigger again a belief adequate for their situation. As our Lord stretched out a hand to Peter, perhaps your word today can help someone who is sinking to continue the task entrusted to him.

Prayer

Oh Lord, may I no longer believe that there are some people who do not have problems with faith and obedience. Help me today to be aware that, for the most part, there are only disciples like me — people for whom faith is at best a sometime thing. Help

30 Days to a New You

me to be the one who can say the word that will enable a brother or sister to believe in his or her own worth once again and in Your love and power.

Journal (my reactions, insights and results)

Parable: Six Priests

Several years ago while leading a conference in Bloomington, Illinois, I suddenly became ill. I had developed all the symptoms that go with flu, including chills and fever. Finally, unable to go on with my responsibilities for leading and speaking, I took to my bed in the men's dormitory.

My sudden illness was announced to those at the conference, and within an hour an amazing parade of people turned up to offer help. The first anointed me with oil for healing — my first experience of this ancient rite of the church. The next one simply wanted to kneel by my bed and offer prayer for me. The third person was a woman doctor who gave concrete medical help. She dosed me with aspirin, took my pulse, and reassured me that in all probability I had a twenty-four-hour flu bug. The fourth person brought me a tray of food which was the last thing in the world I wanted at that time. The fifth person just popped in to express concern and love, while the sixth, and last, was a wonderful Finnish masseuse who sang hymns in her native language while she gave me a massage.

Two things happened. First, I was healed within the hour. I don't know which one of those people was the channel of God's healing, but I suspect they all were used. But even more exciting, I became aware that God was teaching me to receive help from Him through others. Now it has always been much easier for me to give than receive, and that has often caused a block in relationships. I still thank God for the lesson He taught me through my six teachers.

Word for the Day: John 6:5,9,10

> "When Jesus looked up and saw a great crowd coming toward him, he said to Philip, 'Where shall we buy bread for these people to eat?' . . . 'Here is a boy with five small barley loaves and two small fish, but how far will they go among so many?' . . . There was plenty of grass in that place, and the men sat down, about five thousand of them."

Consciousness Raiser and Application

In Jesus' life and ministry there are two constants in His relationships with people. First, Jesus often asked for help. So many encounters that are recorded in the New Testament begin by His request

30 Days to a New You

for a drink or food or lodging or for someone to pray with Him.

Secondly and most surprising, Jesus seemed to ask help of the most unlikely people and expected help from such unlikely sources. In our word for the day, a small boy with only a basket lunch becomes a resource for feeding five thousand people.

With Jesus as your model, try these two constants in your relationships today. Be ready to ask for help, and expect that help from some unlikely sources. In the problems you have today, seek answers from people you would not normally include.

For example, as a parent you might ask your children to help you with some problem that affects the home or even something outside the home. You might be surprised at what this can do for your relationship with them. You might even get some answer that the wisest counselor could not have given. For next to the Lord, who knows you better than your children!

If you are the manager of a department or the head of a business, try consulting someone at a lower level of management for a solution to a plant or office problem. Sometimes the person who works at the bottom of the organizational ladder sees more concretely the real bottlenecks or possibilities.

If you are in some academic center, try asking a student there for an answer to a teaching or administrative problem. A young person might get a new perspective on his or her problem from a senior citizen and vice versa.

Try these two things today, then. Learn to ask for help more readily, and allow God's answer to come from hitherto unsuspected channels. In other words, do not limit the means by which your cry for help can be heard. Let God surprise you, not only with the answer, but with His means of revealing that answer.

Prayer
Lord, help me to believe that You love me and that Your love can only come at the place where I am ready to receive. Beyond that let me know that You have an infinitely creative way of revealing Your will in my life. Let me not despise any one of Your creatures, but honor all people as instruments of Your grace, wisdom, caring, and love.

Journal (my reactions, insights and results)

Parable: The Mediator

'Twas the week before Christmas and all through the bus not a creature was stirring. We were packed in like sardines, with even standing room at a premium as regular commuters vied with last-minute shoppers for space. The road was slippery, traffic was heavy, and the bus was behind schedule. An atmosphere of irritation and gloom prevailed that was anything but a "holiday spirit."

I was standing near the center of the bus, facing sideways to catch the bit of light available for reading. In the seat just below me were two men wearing caps and leather jackets. They seemed somewhat out of place among the crowd of white-collar workers. One was a man of middle years, the other a boy of twenty or so. I assumed they were father and son. Just behind them were two nuns, chatting amiably and glancing from time to time at their open missals.

Suddenly the bus lurched to a stop and, caught off balance, I grabbed for a handhold to keep from falling. In doing so, I struck a glancing blow to the head of the older man seated below. It must have felt like a karate chop!

Immediately I began to apologize and express my hope that he wasn't hurt, but he would not be placated. Instead, he denounced my carelessness in abusive language, especially for reading when I should have been holding on. My attempts to interrupt him and repeat my apology only enraged him further.

At this, the woman standing next to me got into the act. Indignant over the man's attitude, she let him know how difficult it was to be a standee.

"I paid for my seat!" he shouted.

"I paid for a seat too!" she promptly replied.

At that he became more angry than ever. I fully expected him to get up and punch me in the nose. The young man with him tried to calm him down to no avail. Suddenly, with supreme sarcasm, another standee said, loud enough for the entire busload to hear: "Merry Christmas, everybody!"

The grim greeting brought an end to the scene which had involved all those in the immediate area. That is, all except the two nuns. They were busily reading their missals, looking neither right nor left.

Much later at the first major stop, many people got off, including my angry "friend." The young man did not leave with his companion, and I sat down beside him. As soon as I was settled, he smiled and said, "I hope you will forgive him for the way he acted. You really picked the worst possible time to tangle with him. He's a bricklayer, and today he had an accident that almost cost him his hand. The foreman has threatened to fire him. Not only that, but he is having trouble with his wife."

"Is he a friend of yours?" I asked.

The boy shook his head. "I never saw him before. I'm a college student home for the holidays. We just happened to sit next to each other, and he told me his story."

It occurred to me that we had lived through an incident typical of what happens in each of our lives many times a day. The setting may be an office, a home, a factory, a school, a board room, a church, or any of the many backdrops against which we live out our lives. The circumstances may be different, but the cast of characters is the same. There are the offenders (the role I played in this case), the offended (the bricklayer), the "sidetakers" (those who by word or attitude defend or attack either of the antagonists), and lastly, the uninvolved (in this case, the two nuns).

But in the midst of this scene there was also a priest, a mediator — the young student who tried to bridge the gap between the bricklayer and me. Speaking separately to the offended one and the offender, he tried to remove the barriers of misunderstanding.

Word for the Day: Matthew 5:9
> "Blessed are the peacemakers, for they will be called sons of God."

Consciousness Raiser and Application

One of the great mistakes I make in reading the Bible is to try and spiritualize everything I read. Now while there are some tremendously profound words and events that can only be understood through spiritual discernment, most of the Bible contains clear and specific directions that are simple to understand but not easy to do.

The Beatitudes are a prime example of this. One of the Beatitudes is a simple injunction from Jesus to be peacemakers.

What does it mean to be a peacemaker? Well, the definition is not at all complicated. To begin with, it is the opposite of being a troublemaker. A peacemaker is someone who tries to reconcile two people who are having a disagreement. We can be peacemakers and reconcilers for two individuals or two groups in our home, our church, or our school system. One doesn't have to wait to serve at the United Nations and be engaged in the business of reconciling nations to take Jesus' word literally.

And so today, if you are a follower of Jesus Christ and believe in the priesthood of believers, become aware of people in your life who need reconciliation. Probably each has a good reason for disliking or mistrusting or misunderstanding the other. Your job is to begin to prayerfully and lovingly interpret the actions of each to the other in such a way that peace and understanding may result. Perhaps there is no more difficult task than this one that our Lord has given us so clearly. But the simplicity of it is staggering. With His help, you and I can become peace-makers and priests to one another.

Prayer
Lord, give me the audacity to believe that You would have me stand between two unhappy, disagreeing, anxiety-filled, angry people as Your peacemaker. Give me Your Spirit that I might interpret each to the other in the best light. Let me be one who can bring reconciliation between men because You have reconciled me to God through Your life in me.

Journal (my reactions, insights and results)

Parable: The Bus

For many years I traveled to my New York office by bus. The only positive part of that long tedious trip was that I was often able to use the time to get some necessary work done. One day I was especially eager to work on something pressing, and I took a seat over the wheel, hoping that no one would sit next to me, and spread my briefcase and papers on the adjoining seat.

At the last stop before expressing into New York, the seat beside me was the only one unoccupied. Two people got on the bus: a well-dressed young man and a frail and elderly woman, and the young man beat her to the seat.

For several minutes I sat fiercely resenting this young man next to me. But being a Christian means that God deals with our resentments, and I began to lose mine in my concern and compassion for the woman who was having a difficult time staying afoot as the bus lurched about.

30 Days to a New You 171

I began to pray that someone would give her a seat. It was unthinkable that I should give up mine because I had work to do and one cannot work standing up on a bus. Before long, however, the Lord let me know that I was sitting on the answer to my prayer.

Trading my irrelevant prayer for some relevant action, I offered the woman my seat. Then as I stood in the aisle, my focus was once again on the young man sitting just beneath me. In the midst of feeling smug about being both a gentleman and a Christian, I realized what I really needed was a new and right spirit.

Here was a lesson for me in microcosm. In a short space of time I had moved from (1) resentment to (2) concern to (3) irrelevant prayer to (4) relevant action to (5) relevant action with the right spirit.

Word for the Day: Acts 10:9-15, 19, 20

> ". . . Peter went up on the roof to pray. He became hungry and wanted something to eat, and while the meal was being prepared, he fell into a trance. He saw heaven opened and something like a large sheet being let down to earth by its four corners. It contained all kinds of four-footed animals, as well as reptiles of the earth and birds of the air. Then a voice told Peter, 'Get up,

Peter. Kill and eat.'

'Surely not, Lord!' Peter replied. 'I have never eaten anything impure or unclean.'

The voice spoke to him a second time, 'Do not call anything impure that God has made clean.' . . .

While Peter was still thinking about the vision, the Spirit said to him, 'Simon, three men are looking for you. So get up and go downstairs. Do not hesitate to go with them, for I have sent them.'"

Consciousness Raiser and Application

The Bible is the most exciting book in the world to me. Not just because I believe it is the Word of God, but because it is *my* story. All through its pages I keep finding people just like me. If God can work with people like that, love them and use them, then I can take heart and believe that He can love and use me.

Our word for the day comes from the Book of Acts which is an account of the birth and expansion of the Christian church. At this point in the story, Peter had become the acknowledged leader of the early apostles and disciples. All of the believers were looking to Peter for definitive words and actions, for interpretations and new strategies.

Peter's vision occurred while he was visiting in a

home in Joppa where he had just raised a dead girl to life in the name and by the power of Jesus Christ. I am sure Peter was both frightened and humbled at witnessing this miracle, and we are told he returned to the rooftop to pray. In the midst of his prayer a vision came that told him to eat food that no righteous Jew would ever eat.

When a committee came to interrupt his prayers and his spiritual time, the vision had prepared Peter to agree to go with them to the house of a Gentile soldier in Caesarea named Cornelius. What happened there was another miracle. When Peter preached the Gospel to Gentiles for the first time, the Holy Spirit fell on the entire household and new disciples were made.

Today, look for ways that the Holy Spirit might take you from your "spiritual exercises" and give you some specific direction — direction that might seem mundane or trivial or even downright unorthodox or dangerous. Let God interrupt your prayers if He chooses and give you guidance to be obedient in some way.

As you are being interrupted, you may find you have an irritable spirit within you. In this you can certainly identify with Peter and a great number of others since the first century believers. As you set off about your tasks, ask God to put a right spirit within you so that you can be a prepared instrument for doing or being His will in some specific situation. Expect miracles in unexpected places today through your obedience and by God's Spirit.

Prayer
Lord, today I pray that You would deliver me from the temptation of spirituality. Let me know that Your Holy Spirit speaks often in plain, simple, costly, and even repulsive ways. Let me be willing to dirty my hands, to go where I would not choose to go, or to be involved with people whom I have previously despised. Let me be as open to Your new strategy for my life as was Your servant Peter so many years ago.

Journal (my reactions, insights and results)

Modern
Estonian Poetry

ANTHOLOGY OF

Modern
Estonian Poetry

COMPILED AND TRANSLATED BY

William Meesmann
W. K. MATTHEWS

UNIVERSITY OF LONDON

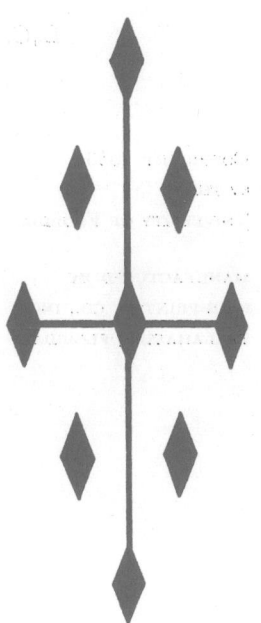

UNIVERSITY OF FLORIDA PRESS
GAINESVILLE
1953

PREFATORY NOTE

THIS BOOK derives for the most part from a manuscript which was completed under the title of *Poets of Renascent Estonia* in 1939 and which would have been published as a de luxe edition with illustrations by an eminent Estonian artist in Tallinn in the following year but for the Soviet annexation of Estonia. Some of the poems it contains have already appeared in print, namely, as illustrations to my articles "The Estonian Sonnet" (*The Slavonic and East European Review* XXV, 64, London, 1946) and "The Background and Poetry of Gustav Suits" (*The American Slavic and East European Review* IX, 2, New York, 1950) and separately in *The American Slavic and East European Review* (Menasha, 1947), in the London publications *Translation* (1947) and *Life and Letters* (LV, No. 122, 1947), and in my anthology *Earthbound: Selected Poems of Bernard Kangro* (Lund, 1951). *Life and Letters* also included a substantial share of the introductory essay "Phases of Estonian Poetry."

Permission to include copyright matter published outside Estonia since loss of independence has been graciously given by Marie Under, Gustav Suits, Artur Adson, Herk Visnapuu (for his uncle, the late Henrik Visnapuu), Pedro Krusten, Hilda Esko-Saks, Karl Ristikivi, Kalju Lepik, Arved Viirlaid, Ivar Grünthal,

Reet Veer-Vellner, and Raimond Kolk, who, as editor of the periodical *Sôna* (Stockholm), has also consented to the publication of my version of a poem by the late Kalju Ahven. To all these ladies and gentlemen, who so readily came to my aid, I offer my sincere thanks, as I do also to Valev Uibopuu, co-editor of *Välis-Eesti* (Stockholm), whose kindness and efficiency helped me to find the present whereabouts of many of them. Lastly I wish to express my profound sense of gratitude to the Directorate of the Eesti Rahvusfond (Estonian National Fund) in Stockholm for providing me with a large number of recently published books and periodicals to assist me in my work and for generously helping to finance the publication of my anthology; to the University of Florida Press for publishing it; and especially to Professors Gustav Suits and Ants Oras for their unfailing interest in my work of fifteen years' standing and for their unselfish and indefatigable efforts to enable me to see it in print at long last.

Blackpool (England), 1953.   W. K. MATTHEWS.

CONTENTS

CONTENTS

ix

CONTENTS

CONTENTS

Phases of Estonian Poetry

I

ESTONIAN FOLKSONG possesses a tradition which appears to go back considerably beyond the thirteenth century, when the Estonian people lost their freedom and were converted by the sword to German Catholicism. The heroic ballads alluded to in medieval Scandinavian sources incline us to conjecture that originally Estonian folksong was sung by minstrels and had a masculine intonation. This would seem to have been lost with loss of independence. The numerous songs which have survived to this day are sung by women and reflect mainly feminine modes of thought and feeling.

Estonian poetry in the narrower sense of this word has not been deeply influenced by folksong, because until recently the nature and significance of the latter were not adequately understood. Even during the period of national awakening (1860-1880), when it was widely imitated, the prevailing romanticism was apt to dilute its racy vitality.

Verse composition in Estonian began without the intervention of folk poetry in the first half of the seventeenth century, when a group of German clergy and teachers in Tallinn, familiar with the discipline of the *leges opitianae*, made flippant and patronising use of the language for occasional verse of no literary merit, and Heinrich Stahl inserted wooden renderings of Lutheran hymns in his *Hand- und Hausbuch für das Fürstentumb Ehsten in Liffland I-II* (1632-1638). The first writer of purely Estonian origin was Käsu Hans, whose arid, but not altogether unpoetical, lament on the destruction of Tartu by the armies of Peter the Great in 1708 (*Oh, ma waene Tardo liin!*) follows the uninspired baroque tradition established by the German versifiers. Even at the beginning of the nineteenth century Estonian poetry was still under German tutelage. The Estophils Heinrich Rosenplänter and J. W. L. von Luce had encouraged their German fellow-countrymen to study Estonian folksongs, old and new, and Count Peter von Manteuffel, Heinrich Wahl, R. J. Winkler, and P. H. von Frey imitated them more or less successfully. Incomparably superior to these well-intentioned poetasters was the promising philologist and poet, Kristjan Jaak Peterson (1801-1822), whose premature death was a grave loss to Estonian poetry. He was of Estonian extraction and one of the first of his nationality to enter Tartu University after the emancipation of the Estonian peasantry from serfdom. This is the earliest significant name in the history of Estonian literature. But Peterson remained entirely unknown until his poetry was disinterred by Gustav Suits at the beginning of this century.

Some decades after Peterson's death Estonian poetry reached sudden romantic pinnacles in the patriotic ardour of Lydia Jannsen (Koidula) and the meditative humanity of F. R. Fählmann and F. R. Kreutzwald. The last is best known as the author of that noble mosaic "The Kalevid"* (*Kalevipoeg*, 1857-1861), which, like the Finnish epic *Kalevala*, became a symbol and buttress of national pride.

Koidula's lyrics and Kreutzwald's epic were the verbal and emotional reflections of a movement which resisted oppression from

* My version of the "Dedication" (Soovituseks) of this poem will be found in *The Slavonic and East European Review* XXIX, 72, London, 1950.

above not with physical force, but with organised knowledge. In the eighteen-sixties begins a brief and hopeful period of national awakening marked by the foundation of Estonian schools, theatres, and literary societies, and by the confident and courageous use of the Estonian vernacular. The national movement, directed against German hegemony, had been supported by the Russian Government. But towards the beginning of the eighteen-eighties this support was withdrawn in the interests of "panslavism." German hegemony was replaced by Russian, and a period of intensive russification set in. The poetry of the period of national awakening (*ärkamisaeg*) survived in epigonic form as variations on receding literary themes: Koidula's fire had sunk to the embers of Jaan Bergmann and M. J. Eisen. The period of russification continued till the revolution of 1905, but more than a decade before this date Estonians had begun to take active measures to protect themselves. The focus of the national movement had now shifted from the south to the north, where it assumed an urban and socialist complexion. But Tartu and the south still remained nationally significant. The oldest surviving Estonian newspaper, "Postman" (*Postimees*), founded by Koidula's father, the author J. W. Jannsen, in 1857, had been taken over by Jaan Tônisson in 1896, and he and his more enlightened colleagues now exercised a steadying influence on the trend of national sentiment.

With the growth of urban nationalism the romantic moods of the period of national awakening gave place to realism, which in literature was reinforced by the spirit of the age and its West European manifestations. The realistic approach is found chiefly in contemporary Estonian prose — in the plays of August Kitzberg and the fiction of Eduard Wilde — but it was not overlooked by the poets of the eighteen-nineties. Even such distinctly romantic temperaments as K. E. Sööt (b. 1862) and Anna Haava (b. 1864) illustrate the formative impingement of realism. The latter, for instance, sets out in the stereotyped Heinesque manner to develop a narrow range of lyrical themes and ends up with free verse and with bolder and richer chords. But it is Juhan Liiv (1864-1913) who shows the impress of the new attitude most clearly. The romantic veneer of his early verse wears off in trenchant satire and tragic introspection. His own mental ailment as much as the spirit of the age determines his inclinations now. Liiv, however, goes beyond realism. His agonies lead him on to neoromanticism and symbolism. Lucid moments during his later years record as in a mirror not only his sufferings, but often enough a synthesis of these with the moral humiliations of his oppressed country. And the longing for physical regeneration echoes in the larger hope of national liberty, which finally speaks with the lips of messianic prophecy.

Juhan Liiv was loved and admired by the writers of the Young Estonia (*Noor-Eesti*) group, the creators of modern Estonian literature. But their youthful enthusiasm seems to have caused him more distress than pleasure. In a poem addressed to his admirers (*Noor-Eestile* "To Young Estonia") Liiv urges them not to honour *him*, but to choose as leader a man "grown up in light" and conscious of his aims, and as such better able to show them the way. This poem belongs to the year of the first Russian revolution; 1905 also dates a revolution in Estonian poetry.

II

Though the revolution of 1905 was suppressed in blood, its effect soon afterwards was to check the progress of russification and to bring economic and cultural relief to the Estonian people. The growth of material prosperity was accompanied by a considerable growth in the numbers of the Estonian educated class, and freedom of expression revived the party spirit and political journalism. The new tolerance towards ideas and ideologies favoured the development of a national culture. Schools and universities filled with Estonians, the publishing house "Estonian Literature" (*Eesti*

Kirjanduse Selts) and the Estonian National Museum (*Eesti Rahva Muuseum*) were founded, the Tartu and Tallinn theatres ("Vanemuine" and "Estonia") opened larger premises, and translations of good books multiplied.

Even before the revolution of 1905 Estonian national consciousness had found expression in secret political and literary societies at the gymnasia (grammar schools), especially in Tartu, Pärnu, and Kuressaare. In Tartu, Gustav Suits, then a pupil of the local gymnasium, founded a society called Friends of Literature (*Kirjanduse sôbrad*), which between 1901 and 1902 published three numbers of the album "Irradiations" (*Kiired*), containing contributions by writers of the older generation as well as by adolescent authors. The object of "Irradiations" was to promote original literature and criticism and the translation of important books from foreign languages. After the appearance of the third number the publication was officially prohibited, but the activity of the youths continued in secret. In 1902 the nationalist literary society, The Estonian Sower (*Eesti Külvaja*), was inaugurated and before long had amassed a library containing the works of Nietzsche, Tolstoy, Ibsen, Darwin, Brandes, Marx, and Kautsky. This society was unearthed and disbanded by the police, but, like its predecessor, soon transformed itself into another. The new society came into existence in 1903 under the name Union (*Ühisus*) and had manifestly literary leanings, its members being interested chiefly in French literature. During 1903 Suits was in Finland, where he made the acquaintance of Finnish writers and conceived the idea of issuing a literary publication modelled on the "Young Finland" (*Nuori Suomi*) album, to celebrate the centenary of Kreutzwald's birth. The idea materialised only in the spring of 1905, when the first "Young Estonia" (*Noor-Eesti*) album appeared. In the meantime Suits had revived the Friends of Literature society with the help of Friedebert Tuglas (Mihkelson), Johannes Aavik, and Bernhard Linde, and with Villem Ridala (Grünthal), then living in Kuressaare, as a sort of corresponding member. These afterwards

adopted the name Young Estonia, and the most important movement in Estonian literature was inaugurated.

In the first Young Estonia album Suits wrote: "More culture!
More European culture! Let us be Estonians and at the same time
let us become Europeans." These exhortations came ultimately to
represent the aims of the Estonian intelligentsia not merely in literature, but in politics, for Young Estonia was much more than a
literary movement. Its literary bias, however, was strong. The
study of European, especially French, literature concentrated attention on problems of expression and led to a determined effort
to reform and enrich the Estonian language, to cultivate style,
and to foster and develop literary criticism. The philological side
of the effort was ably carried out by Aavik; the critical, by Suits.
In his essays "Aims and Views" (*Sihid ja vaated*, 1906) the latter
emphasises the significance of the individual as against the national and, following Nietzsche, demands a maximum of moral
liberty. But not until the appearance of the second Young Estonia
album in 1907 are these views illustrated in full. The second album
resurrects the poetry of the individualist K. J. Peterson and offers
significant contributions by such leaders of the movement as
Tuglas and Suits. The third album (1909) widens the breach with
the past by offering three naturalistic poems by Jaan Oks and
translations of the French decadents from Baudelaire to Verlaine.
The individualism and aestheticism of the movement is sym-
bolised in the heroine of Aavik's story "Ruth." From now on the
cult of form predominates, and the remaining Young Estonia albums (the fourth appeared in 1912, the fifth in 1915) are con-
secrated to it. The individualist bent of the Young Estonia group
brought it into conflict with conservatives who viewed its criticism
and practice as revolutionary. But its influence on the young was
complete. To these it brought contacts with new worlds and new
modes of thinking. Thanks to Young Estonia, West European literature became familiar to the responsive and appreciative among
the Estonian intelligentsia.

The Young Estonia movement was eclectic, favouring no particular literary inspiration, but drawing sustenance from several. Yet its general tenor was neoromantic and symbolistic. These adjectives fully qualify the poetry of Suits, and the first may be confidently applied to the tranquil nature poems of Ridala. Symbolism blended with impressionism also characterises the contemporary lyrics of Ernst Enno, but this poet held aloof from clique and movement and cultivated an hermetic individualism.

The external influences which affected the work of the Young Estonia poets were mainly French and Italian. Baudelaire, Verlaine, and Verhaeren appealed to Suits; Carducci and d'Annunzio to Ridala. Such influences favoured the cult of form and style. And the exquisite technique of the Romance poets inspired Aavik's and Ridala's attempt to "renovate" the mother tongue. These, with Suits and the representative of imaginative prose, Friedebert Tuglas, raised Estonian literature to a level of distinction. Their work was concentrated into a period covering just over a decade, between two revolutions.

III

At the peak of its development the Young Estonia movement was interrupted by the outbreak of the First World War, which put a temporary end to literary activity in Estonia. When the war and the Russian revolution of 1917 had prepared the way for the Estonian war of independence, interest in literature immediately revived. The signal for renewed literary activity coincided with the return of Tuglas and Wilde from exile in the spring of 1917. Soon afterwards Tuglas, with the poets Artur Adson, Marie Under, and Henrik Visnapuu, and the novelist August Gailit, formed the literary society "Siuru" (so named after a legendary bird in "The Kalevid"). Most of these authors had already contributed to the Young Estonia albums, so that their debut in the Siuru albums had all the characteristic marks of maturity. Three such albums appeared between 1917 and 1919, and the items included in them illustrate the salient features of the Young Estonia movement, namely, aestheticism, individualism, fantasy, and the cult of form. The repressions of the war and revolution years were now followed by the inevitable moral reaction. Visnapuu in "Amores" (1917) and Marie Under in her "Sonnets" (*Sonetid*, 1917) gave candid expression to erotic sentiment in their pursuit of egocentric pleasures. The Siuru albums too emphasised the individual and his instincts in transparent terms, though these often enough were borrowed from other languages. A peculiar fondness for exotic words led to the overloading of Estonian with grotesque alien doublets. Another feature of Siuru poetry was a tendency to enlarge the individual into the social. This tendency became general after the liquidation of the Siuru group in 1919. Two years later most of the members of Young Estonia and Siuru combined to form the cultural and political association Tarapita, to wage war against the stubborn anticultural elements in Estonian society.

Ultraindividualism in politics, morals, and literature exerted an influence on language. Aavik's inventiveness went beyond the innovations that are now usually accepted. Some of his suggestions read like the fantastic and grotesque stories he was in the habit of translating to illustrate his lexical principles. But fundamentally his reforms were sane and sound, and because of them the Estonian language has become a vigorous and adaptable medium of expression.

IV

A tendency to substitute realistic for romantic moods is evident in the later practice of members of the Siuru group and in the social interests of its metamorphosis Tarapita. It is even more apparent in the work of certain hangers-on of the movement, though these remain romanticists at heart.

A thoroughgoing reaction to romanticism could obviously come only from a younger generation, to whom war and revolution and their emotional reflexes were mainly hearsay. Such a reaction is illustrated by a short-lived periodical called "Literary Orbit" (*Kirjanduslik Orbiit*, 1929-1930), which received contributions mainly from prose authors. The poets of the Orbit movement, including Juhan Sütiste, were more robust than their predecessors and took little or no interest in refinements of language and in the individualist pose. They were drawn to slum life and to the cause of the inarticulate and levelling masses. Like the English left-wing poets of the nineteen-thirties, they had a profound social consciousness. But unlike these, they largely succeeded in suppressing their egoisms and in harnessing their talents to the service of their country.

The depersonalisation of poetry was apparently carried too far because of the fluency and lack of self-criticism characteristic of the Literary Orbit poets. A still younger body of authors had meanwhile appeared. These, like the Young Estonia and Siuru poets, had been brought up on European literature, but they did not constitute a group and were free from the Bohemian snobbery of the aesthetes. For international culture, whether aesthetic, like that of the Young Estonia and Siuru, or sociological, like that of the Literary Orbit, they substituted a national culture, and for the impersonal art of the last-mentioned, a personal art chastened by study and comparison. Native as well as foreign influences were not lacking in their work. The subtleties of Suits and the alien irradiation of the French and Russian Symbolists had left felicitous traces. There was a general refinement in the use of language and more often than not the presence of a prosodic conscience. Yet the technical acquisitions had been critically sifted and applied to the sober reproduction of the prevailing emotional atmosphere. This reflected the pessimism of the times — as apparent in Estonia as elsewhere — and a new romantic radiance. Professor Ants Oras, the poet-translator, collected and commended the work of the younger generation in his anthology "Logomancers" (*Arbujad,*

1938). The title suggests a common purpose, perhaps till then subconscious, and certainly unformulated in a manifesto or embodied in a coterie. But the illustrative material shows how strikingly diverse and individually aloof were the new talents. Uku Masing's Scriptural and Protestant mysticism is unique, and the Blok-like pessimism of Heiti Talvik has nothing in common with the subdued nature-love of Bernard Kangro, or the witty reserve of Betti Alver with the vernal spontaneity of Kersti Merilaas. The work of all these and of several others found Estonian poetry emerged from the pains of rebirth and advancing towards the promise of a strenuous maturity.

V

This was the Estonian literary scene and these were most of its principal actors up to the middle of that fateful June of 1940, when the sudden and bewildering irruption of Soviet forces and the Communist *coup d'état,* which quickly followed, put an end to Estonian political and literary independence, and the activities of Estonian writers were curtailed and restricted by the imposition of Leninist standards from above. The years 1940 and 1941 were relatively uncreative. Literature had been diverted into the official channel of socialist realism, and such writers as had previously shown interest in proletarian themes either continued to give expression to this interest or, where it had become dormant, revived it.

The Soviet occupation led ultimately to the liquidation of the Estonian publishing enterprises Estonian Literature (*Eesti Kirjanduse Selts*) and Young Estonia (*Noor-Eesti*), which were replaced by the State Literary Centre (*Riiklik Kirjanduskeskus*) with its various departments. The magazines "Creative Art" (*Looming*) and *Varamu,* the latter as "Pentagon" (*Viisnurk*), were converted into instruments of Soviet propaganda, and both ceased publication with the German invasion of 1941.

On the outbreak of hostilities between the U.S.S.R. and Germany, Estonia, like the other two Baltic States, at first became a battlefield, then came under German occupation, and was finally incorporated in the newly constituted province of Ostland. Under the Germans, whose arrival had raised hopes of a freer creative activity, national expression was for the most part muzzled, as it had been under the Communists, and the Soviet-sponsored literary movement remained in abeyance. The years 1941-1944 proved to be as disappointing as the first experience of foreign occupation. Like most of their compatriots, those Estonian authors who had not fled with the Russians lived on in a state of passive resistance. Their difficulty may be seen, for instance, in the experience of Betti Alver, whose newest book was vetoed by the German censor. Visnapuu, however, was allowed to edit the purely literary magazine "Rainbow" (*Ammukaar*), of which three numbers were printed at irregular intervals between 1942 and 1944, and the publishing house "Young Estonia" was given the opportunity of renewing its activities, but these resulted in the publication of nothing significant and came to an end with the second coming of the Communists in 1944.

The Soviet regime and its author-representatives were restored to power in the latter half of 1944, and the conditions prevailing in 1940-1941 reappeared. When the second Soviet occupation seemed inevitable, Estonian writers at home were faced with the choice of Soviet ideology or exile, and this led ultimately to the schism which now divides Estonia into two literary camps.

Contemporary Estonian literature has two foci — one at home and the other abroad, the latter partly in Sweden, partly in Germany. The German centre, which was intellectually less important than the Swedish from the outset, has been gradually disintegrating with the emigration of Estonian "displaced persons" to other countries. Its characteristic representative Henrik Visnapuu, champion of East Baltic and "Balto-Scandian" unity, died recently in the United States, and others, including a small group of young poets headed by Arved Viirlaid, are in England. Even the Swedish centre has latterly lost some of its younger members; nevertheless it still remains, as it was in 1944, the nucleus of independent Estonian culture. Stockholm is now the home of nearly all the major Estonian poets, including Suits and Marie Under, and publishes nearly all the principal Estonian periodicals. Here, after a short spell in Helsinki (1944), the literary periodical "Estonian Creative Art" (*Eesti Looming*) appeared in 1945-1946 as a worthy successor to the great Tartu monthly. The editorial board included Suits, Ants Oras, and Karl Ristikivi, and the expressed aim of the periodical was contained in a modification of the Young Estonia slogan "Let us be Estonians and become Europeans" (*olgem eestlased ja saagem eurooplasteks*) to "Let us be Estonians and Europeans" (*olgem eestlased ja eurooplased*), in order to meet the inevitable demand of a resuscitated independent Estonia for national and international culture. "Estonian Creative Art" ceased publication in 1946, and for almost two years after that no periodical of quite the same order and purpose was published to serve the intellectual needs of the Estonian community in Stockholm. At last, in 1948, the urgent demand for a literary and learned periodical was met by the issue of the rather bulky stencilled publication "Word" (*Sôna*). It was the organ of a group of writers and artists known as *Tuulisui*, and two of its three editors were the poets Raimond Kolk and Kalju Lepik. It was avowedly an attempt to fill the gap left by the disappearance of "Estonian Creative Art" and was intended to provide "a free forum" for Estonian authors, critics, and scholars, its limits being determined not by point of view, but by literary and intellectual quality. True to its programme, "Word" did not confine itself exclusively to Estonian interests, but introduced its readers to contemporary West European ideas and letters. "Word" appeared in Stockholm and gave ample scope for self-expression to young poets as well as to those with an established reputation. An even more important literary periodical began to appear in May, 1950, under the title of "Scorched Earth" (*Tulimuld*) and the editorship of Bernard Kangro, who in his preface to the first number declared that the periodical was intended to "preserve and develop Estonian culture, to unite all those Estonians who desire culture, and to rouse Estonian youth and bind it to its ancient and vigorous national culture." Like "Word," this periodical prints not only original imaginative literature, but critical articles and documented scholarly essays. It represents the latest development in the extraordinary and almost incredible literary activity, which only about seven per cent of the total population of Estonia has made possible.

This activity was stimulated to some extent by the Estonian publishing house Orto, which began work at Vadstena (Sweden) in 1944 and has since then regularly issued reprints of Estonian classics, as well as new writing. Nevertheless it would be a mistake to imagine that most of the Estonian verse published in Sweden bears the Orto imprint. A great deal of it has appeared in periodicals, and several books of verse, for instance Bernard Kangro's, have been printed privately. As striking as the number and artistic appearance of the many verse-collections are their high average level of achievement and the variety of talent displayed in them. Older authors, like Suits, Marie Under, and Artur Adson, continue to publish characteristic work in periodicals and, apart from Suits, whose "Fire and Wind" (*Tuli ja tuul*) came out in 1950, have not had a book printed for several years. In contrast to them, Bernard Kangro published six collections between 1945 and 1952, and the much younger Kalju Lepik four between 1946 and 1951. The latter has already established himself as an original poet, and there are several other contemporaries, for instance Raimond Kolk, the dialect poet, Ivar Grünthal, and Reet Veer (Vellner), in whose work there are definite signs of personal and poetical integrity.

In Kangro's periodical "Scorched Earth" Henrik Visnapuu is mentioned as its American editor. Till quite recently this versatile and productive poet was one of the forces of Estonian literary activity in Germany. Visnapuu was important also as an organiser, for it was he who founded the German branch of the World Society of Estonian Literature (*Ülemaailmaline Eesti Kirjanduse Selts*) at the IRO camp at Geislingen (Württemberg) in 1949, with the object of "organising nationally-minded Estonian culture-workers all over the world" in an effort to preserve and develop the national tradition. The literary reflection of this undertaking was the quarterly symposium "The Gatherer" (*Koguja*), one of whose editors was Pedro Krusten, who is now in the U.S. This publication reflects the term rather than the peak of an intense literary activity, which, astonishingly enough, was not brought to a standstill even by the increased cost of book production resulting from the currency reform in Germany. Karl Kesa's substantial and well-printed anthology "Blue Weave" (*Sinikangas*, 1948), covering Estonian poetry from K. J. Peterson to Raimond Kolk, may be taken as a salient illustration of the spirit of perseverance which has stimulated this activity and successfully overcome all obstacles and difficulties. This anthology also represents a persistent and salutary demand for poetry among Estonians in exile.

Such a demand is the best augury for the development of expatriate Estonian poetry, though the exodus of Estonians from Germany overseas may exercise an injurious effect in the long run, unless the Estonian groups in the Americas and the Antipodes can survive as cultural units. Indeed, the very existence of an Estonian literature in exile very largely depends on the existence of a relatively numerous and educated reading public. The numbers of the Estonian community in Europe were highest in 1945-1946 and since then have gradually declined. The decline has led to depletion and diminution of the main centres and to the establishment of new ones elsewhere. But even this inevitable process of decentralisation can be counterbalanced to some extent by active collaboration among the various scattered centres, and realisation of such a possibility has led to the multiplication of branches of national organisations like the Estonian National Fund and the World Society of Estonian Literature, to the revival of the Young Estonia (*Noor-Eesti*) Press in Stockholm, and to the foundation of the very enterprising Estonian Authors' Cooperative Society (*Eesti Kirjanike Kooperativ*), which has already published an outstanding series of original prose works and some books of verse in Lund.

The strength of Estonian poetry in exile at the present time resides in its possession of a notable body of authors, including several of those who were actively associated with its most significant modern movements. Its weakness is mostly a function of time, for without a new generation to cultivate it, this poetry and, in fact, expatriate Estonian literature in general can hardly be expected to survive. Naturally enough its attitude has been conservative rather than progressive, for it has tended on the whole to reproduce the models and manners of a decade ago. This has been acutely felt by the editors of "Word," and one of them, Ilmar Talve, has expressly urged the desirability of adapting the prewar literary tradition to changing needs. Here we have a sane approach to national literature in exile which refuses to neglect the tendency to change characteristic of all living literatures.

Sulle Emamaa, kes olid
Võitva päeva kõrgustesse
Kaduviku tuha valust
Tõusnud tulilinnuna,
Sulle jälle tuhka langend,
Sulle uute tiibe ootel.

J UHAN LIIV

The Hooded Forest Was Murmuring

The hooded forest was murmuring
With tongues of tried sorcery;
Deep in my childhood its rumour
Bent shadows over me.

The dark mysterious rumour
Outstrips the faltering years;
My spirit is heavy with grieving,
And my eyes are spent with tears.

One Word Was Spoken

One word was spoken.
The hour
And one word spoken
Had power
To unseal heaven and fashion
White wings of exultant passion.

One word was spoken.
Unkindness
Drew unwinged grief from
My blindness.
Just two words — magic lips parted —
Brought High Heart down to low-hearted.

Petals of Pure Snow

Petals of pure snow,
Falling softly,
Flutter as they blow
Earthwards softly.

Lingering on their way,
Spinning softly,
Now they seem to say:
"Softly! . . . Softly!"

Would they banish pain?
Heart, beat softly!
Light and this must wane
Nightwards softly.

Our Room Has Soot-blackened Rafters

Our room has soot-blackened rafters
That loom through the smoky air,
And the cobwebs are dense in its corners,
And cockroaches scuttle there.

What has it not heard and witnessed!
What tongue shall ever tell?

2

But pain draws speaking shadows,
And the speaking face can spell.

It has seen such tears and trials
And heard so much bitterness,
And shared with silences only
Drawn agonies of distress.

Our room has soot-blackened rafters.
This age has such rafters too
That stare down on tangled fetters.
Ah, if it could speak to you!

Early Flower

I came on a wood-flower swaying
On its stalk where the leaves lay sere.
It seemed too frail for staying;
The spring was still new to the year.

And I looked at the delicate flower,
The petals more subtle than art;
And time seemed to forfeit its power
As spring put out leaves in my heart.

Frost

The white-furred woods are still as death;
Light presses crimson into day;
And through the air, obscuring sight,
Keen north-blown crystals spill in spray.
Then out of stillness towards the light
Long harsh throats bell in counterchange,

Dinning the frozen rout of night.
Again the woods grow still as death,
And dawn is gathered into day.

Care

Care, your eyes are strange as unsounded night,
And your cradle is silk, your singing soft.
And how soft, my love, your quiet hand, how light,
As you rock me here singing cradle-songs,
Singing lullabies till you lull me quite!

I awake and go seeking quietude
Far from you where firs hang their branches low,
But your eyes are wide and they see me go,
And they follow me wheresoever I go,
Like a trapper bent on hurried spoor in snow.
And with snare held firm underneath your arm,
You will stop and stare as if you meant no harm,
Eye enquiring: "Why, surely I have known you!
And your secrets too!" But you will not forego
What is yours to take, a spider blurred to view,
Waiting patiently for its food.
So your ambushed eyes will not let me go,
Or else I would escape where there is none to know
You, Care.

I Would Take a Garland of Flowers

I would take a garland of flowers
And bind you with its mirth,
And furl you in its fragrance,
Estonia's orphaned earth.

4

I would take the azure of heaven,
And the brilliance of risen light,
And the colours of dawn and setting,
And crown you in all men's sight.

I would take the bands of affection,
Of honour and loyalty,
And fold you in their comfort
To still your agony.

I would take blood's sacred meshes
And the strong heart's every strand,
And brace you with their valour,
Unfortunate Motherland.

ANNA HAAVA*

Once Only

Once only shall the heart's true passion
Know the pure ecstasy of love,
Once only this miraculous flower
Mirror the mystery from above.

The love that fails, the love that withers
Beyond the reach of eye and mind,
And changes with the changing passions
Differs not in degree, but kind.

Once only shall the heart's true passion
Know love, and then eternity
Draw limits, for there is no power
To alter love's divine decree.

* Pseudonym of Anna Rosalie Haavakivi.

J AAN LÔO

All Souls' Day

Today is All Souls' Day.
Today I shall share them who made me by stages
And brought me out of the dusk of the ages,
The beloved dead who stood each at his station,
Defended and tended our homeland and nation.
Come, all of you, now. You are welcome here;
For all my torches are burning clear;
There is song and feasting and an open door,
And the straw is freshly strewn on the floor.
They have heard my call to return and arise
From their graves as a body with seeing eyes —
My distant forebears from lands of yore:
The hunter and fisher from the Volga shore,
Those who burnt for seed in a Muroma* glade,
Who know where the Kungla† gold is laid,
Who were men-at-arms in the conquering host

* An East Finnic area which probably lay west of present-day Mordvinia, in Central Russia.
† The Estonian Eldorado.

That reached Estonia's Baltic coast,
And those who fell in the last fierce fight,
And those who perished in the slave's long night.
These shadows now fill my house and home
And the courtyard under the November dome.
Eat of the proffered fare at your leisure;
Drink the brown ale from the foaming measure.
Send good hap to my ploughing and sowing;
Prosper endeavour and shelter my growing
People; and dower my sons with passion
And thought for the width and the weal of the homeland,
That this soil which has drunk your perspiration
And your blood shall be saved from violation.
And lastly —
If ever Estonia's sun should dwindle,
Be fleet to her aid like a storm in spring
And sweep her clear of all betrayers,
Oppressors, and flayers;
And, decked in your honour, a grateful race
Shall kindle your lights in every place.

ERNST ENNO

Homesickness

Now white at home the clover stars our meadows,
And the winds blossom in its breath;
But here I long, and tears fall in the shadows.

A slow white road winds through the brilliant day
Into blue woods where solemn whispers stray,
And unseen hands in birchen boughs keep strumming
A silver song to hasten my home-coming.

But here my longings weep among the shadows
For the white perfume of those far-off meadows.

At Sermon Time

Fragrance of mowing blows from fields of hay;
Echoes seek in woods for the light heart of birds;
Pollen drifts from the gilded leas;
Earth is immersed in pure light.

Buzzing of bees in birch and linden-tree;
Father's words are treading the furrows of God;
But my hearing grows blunt and stale;
Only a legend remains.

Woodsprite comes soft-foot from the levelled fields,
Ravenstone* held hard in his moss-covered grip,
And he thrusts the stone in my heart,
Leaving it ponderous there.

Kiln Room

They call you slightingly a dingy smoke-stained den,
Yet you have looked upon their myriad changing faces
And through the centuries have harboured their strong men.
Child's touch and trial singled out your secret places;
Their fraying griefs no less than gales have made you gray;
And in your flooring linger care's assembled traces.

But hid inside your log and stone, a humble ray
Sprung from warm ash has flickered comfortingly tender
And led them with thin music into the tall day.
Their gratitude would surely see you crowned with splendour.

Gray Song

They caged me, and no one would save me
In the far unhappy years.
They caged me, and no one would save me;

* *Kaarnakivi* or *korbikivi*, a stone of magical properties mentioned in Estonian folk-tales. V. Ridala has a ballad on the subject (see "Korbikivi" in his collection *Sinine kari* "Blue Herd").

My singing, they said, had enslaved me;
And I laboured with desolate tears.

O Sun, why will you still call me?
My music is barren as night.
O Sun, why will you still call me?
The bent steep tracks appal me,
And the stakes that ridge the light.

Where weels of gray song are swirling
I would stay till time is shed —
Where weels of gray song are swirling
And word-straws catching and curling
In a nerveless round of the dead.

She Came

She came, and looked at me kindly,
But not a word would she say.
She came, and looked at me kindly,
And then she hastened away.

I rose and followed the footprints
She had left behind in her flight.
I rose and followed her footprints,
And came to the mansion of Night.

"Night, tell me," I said, "where my love is.
Perhaps you have word for me."
"Night, tell me," I said, "where my love is."
But the dark night could not see.

Night stood there and looked at me strangely;
She was bound with a heavy chain.

Night stood there and looked at me strangely,
And I went on my way again.

And always I sought for those footprints
Till I deemed that my quest was won.
And always I sought for those footprints,
And I reached the court of the Sun.

"Sun, tell me," I said, "where my love is.
Perhaps you have something to tell."
"Sun, tell me," I said, "where my love is."
But the sun seemed bound by a spell.

The sun, he looked at me gravely;
So grave are those who know.
The sun, he looked at me gravely,
Till I felt that I must go.

And I went, and sought unhoping
Where I had not sought before,
And I found that the feet I was trailing
Led up to my own soul's door.

The Wind Sang

"In my free spaces earth springs blue and white,"
The wind sang happily the whole night through —
The wind behind the bigging in an aery
Of leaves, and I, as on the edge of faery,
Had to step secretly and softly all night through.

Wind, friendly wind, and you are singing still;
Wind, there behind the bigging all night through?
The blue-white earth is still your strings' tried passion,

And the clear nocturne wakes in the one fashion
A happiness of leaves the whole night through.

Wind, friendly wind, the old tree stands in chains;
The spaces that were free are magic-bound;
A thousand fields resound with orphans' dirges;
The ways break sheer where barren water surges;
The blue-white earth behind the wall is magic-bound.

O way of flesh, weary with bends of pain,
Not you, the solitary wind is free,
As then, behind the bigging in an aery
Of leaves. And somewhere now, emerged from faery,
And with the lips of sleep sings fantasy.

Shadow

The train raced through the sunlight;
The pitch of words was drowned;
And noise of trenchant movement
Remained the only sound.

Each all at once grew silent,
Alone with glass and beam,
And with each other's silence,
And with a budding dream.

I do not now remember
When all this was and where;
But each new glance struck fire,
And fresh leaves hung on air.

She sat there in her corner,
A stranger without name,

And May's clear fingers fashioned
A shadow edged with flame.

I felt an exultation,
As when the spirit stirs,
And saw my own black shadow
Poised there, how close to hers!

So shadow faced black shadow,
And face was close to face.
Ah, what delight of beauty!
How piercing May's green grace!

O happiness and beauty,
And metal pounding air!
I do not now remember
When all this was and where.

Do Not Ask Me

Do not ask me where I wandered,
Or the lands from which I journey;
It was not my wish to wander,
Or my heart's desire to journey.

Hindrances there were a hundred,
Littered obstacles a thousand;
Under me the wain was sorrow,
And the horse was Heed-the-Warning;
I myself the dreary burden.

Who Is It That Damps Our Day?

Sister, what stifling walls! I long to be out there:
My heart is an echo to cries.
Sister, this dreariness! I'll think myself out there,
For none comes to help us rise.

Oh, I have heard there is a world there and freedom,
The freedom entailed as our share;
But alas! evil blight has fallen in my dreaming,
And nothing seems left but despair.

Sister, the home we have, how pinched it is growing,
And the walls how clammy with clay!
Out where the winds stir a dry cross stands warden.
Who is it that damps our day?

Marie Under

Ecstasy

Ah, earthly life burns in a myriad splendours
Not even death's dark hazard can destroy.
I yield, a willing prisoner, to joy;
I never sorted with discreet pretenders.
And as the shaken glaucous wave engenders
Spindrift, so my green falling silks deploy
A froth, and all is stripped to the last toy,
And, caught in ecstasy, my sense surrenders.

Why does the blossom wanton in the light,
The blue horizon lure me to its border?
My body too is of their bent and order:
My every nerve vibrates to rapt delight,
And I distrain my life of its last treasure
As if my mounting days had brimmed their measure.

Autumn Tempest

Listen, the loud-mouthed tempest is clamouring and raving,
Whirling through woodlands and trumpeting high in the tree-tops,
Filling the birds in the branches with quakings of terror,
Lashing the juniper scrub and the tattered dry bushes,
Whistling through undulant thin-bearded stretches of pasture,
Breaking and flinging aside the frost-withered flowers,
Ravening and raging and howling — a wolf in the stubble.

Skywards ascends an unceasing lament from the forest:
Spruces and birches and pines moan loudly for mercy,
Only to crash at a blow from their fierce assailant.
He, with a victor's heart, spurs onwards in triumph,
Laughing an evil laugh as he jingles his rowels,
Tramples on tree-stumps and tosses the far-fallen fir-crests —
King with the iron hands, black autumn tempest.

Night

Over the garden the moon's tide tumbles;
Shrubs are shaken by gusts and tremblings;
Pathways ribbon with sudden dissemblings
Towards the threshold where false foot stumbles.
Out of the soil of midnight, tender,
Lift my arms' white tendrils and, weaving,
Motion to someone shadowy and absent,
Someone who lingers somewhere, perhaps may not be existent.

Oh, do I fear the days of torrid splendour,
Nights full of flowers? Oh, do I fear when I see that
These would not yield to the ultimate depths of my choosing?
My heart is breaking little by little,

17

As a ripe pomegranate, skin parched brittle,
Breaks: full loving is prelude to losing.

Cords are unknotted, the covers have parted,
And I rise winged from where I have smarted.
Oh, do I fear now what heart discloses,
All these desires in fevered legions?
And shall I gather the pure cold roses,
Open and waiting in those white regions,
Towards which the days have died and the nights have faded,
And my blue sail wafts a burning soul that has loved as they did?

Summer Memory

The door ajar, I stood at point of day
Tiptoe for you and with awakened eyes,
The sun's gold slipper trod the gravelled way,

The grasses spilled their dews in glad surprise —
And then you came out of a mist of flowers
That clung and swayed like knots of butterflies!

When afterwards we two in softened hours
Walked through the fields of rye all red for reaping,
I felt as if my heart obeyed new powers:

The old in me seemed either dead or sleeping,
And as I glimpsed the poppies' fluttering fire,
An eager pleasure set my pulses leaping,
And you, these sang, could give me my desire.

Twilit City

I walk deep snowy ways in light that blends
Shapes with its silver dust. The clouds are wearing
Chaplets of lilac where the sky wall ends.

In front a row of mounds squats blankly staring,
And, far behind, a dome of copper glows,
And marshalled ranks of casement squares are flaring.

The belfry clock's round visage leers and blows
Puffs of ironic laughter, lightly falling,
And through my sense a subtle strangeness flows.
The clock strikes . . . Do I hear a cuckoo calling?

Nostalgia

When evening culls me like a flower,
Severs hand from hand, foot from the meadow,
Poring eyes from print, hope from the saddened hour
That escorts the sun into maternal shadow —

I still linger, the play done, unheeded and belated.
Ah, how soon the sun is made a speck, the glad day rust,
And sealed vision has annihilated
Lamp and moon and stars! The vanquished world lies prone
    in dust.

From the peg my slight frock hangs as if decaying,
And my shoes, unlatched from life and motion, fall;
Tables, chairs — the very room seems swaying
In collapse; but, ruin-bred, the soul grows tall.

19

Loosed from the fatigue of trammelled limbs and living,
How it pauses, waiting sadly gay yet free,
And at length, escaped from time's usurious giving,
Reaches, stripped of death, into a green eternity.

Home-love shapes from yearnings blent with pain and bitter:
Like a candle-flame it trembles in a glory
And, impatterned by the sacred glitter
Of pure wings, is set into seraphic story.

Mardus*

Once more the swollen streams of blood are failing;
The broken limbs regain their pristine powers,
And ruin rises up with plank and paling.

Fed on brains' phosphorus-gold in darkened hours,
Earth turfs anew to suit the children's laughter
And heels. And blood has fashioned happy flowers

For innocent hands. But under roof and rafter
The hanging Christ still droops in bloodless sorrow,
And mothers pause to weep for the hereafter.

And in the night what witness of to-morrow?

Blizzard

Oh, this spell of misery,
Cold with sleet and hailstone-gritty!

* The herald voice of disaster and death in Estonian folklore.

Birds that flew across the lea
Beat their wings and pipe for pity.

Growling came the shaggy blizzard;
And the trees, suspecting danger,
Bent their backs before the stranger,
Felt the mace-strokes of the wizard.

Shrubs, disburgeoned without warning,
Droop in mourning.
Oh, who sent this wintry rigour,
Sapping plants of their green vigour?

Snow like ragged linen blanches
Twigs and branches;
Window-panes are splashed to streaming;
And the heart is roused from dreaming.

Oh, begone now,
Spare the teeming
Season, motley-coated ranter,
Many-minded gallivanter!

At the Window

Hooked boughs caught the moonlight's shimmer
As we bade each other good-bye.
I sent you out towards the sky
And a waiting silver-blue glimmer.

I watched you when we had parted:
Mouth grieved as you turned to look round.
Ah, could you have uttered a sound
That had told what your silence imparted.

How gaunt were the linden-trees!
Their leaves, trodden soft, had blackened.
You traced out our haunts by degrees;
Your vision and love had not slackened.

Our fields, once high in flower,
All blue in the saffron hazes,
Were abridged to vaporous mazes,
How lonely at that lonely hour!

Long meadows of fescue-grass
And their fragrance lay far from here.
Ah, distance and things that pass —
These airs were not new to my ear.

The ring of the marshes was growing.
You thought of my dog at the gate,
And it seemed to welcome and wait,
And bark with the pleasure of knowing.

I felt you must surely return;
But no, you slowly descended,
Your back bent. The willows ended,
And then came a sudden turn.

You became quite puny and spineless.
Could that tiny black speck be you?
And how soon you were hidden from view!
The way towards the moon ran signless.

Sharp tears crept into my lashes.
As one begging grace will pray,
I prayed. Nothing fell but flashes
From the moon and the Milky Way.

Moon of the Dead

From a tree the moon hangs raw.
Frothy blood
Flecks the steep flow of the water.
In the fall's enormous maw
Seethes a coiled and slimy cud.
Strain your hearing!
Sounds as of a distant slaughter
Mingle, bleak in horror, nearing
Like a sinister black flood.

Agony haunts crofts and fallows.
Strain your hearing!
Orphans' weeping, widows' wailing,
Violated girls' shrill error —
With all these the winds are loud, the night with terror.

See, the mill, stopped in mid-sailing,
Shapes a gallows.
Surely those are shin-bones clacking,
Ribs and spines with signs of racking?
Pulse and heart are near to dying.
Does the soul, when it shall sever
From the blood, become a crying?
Is there not a place where sorrow
Could be hid, where it could borrow
Comfort in the midst of sighing?
Or will it despair for ever
Here between the earth and sky?

Is there no refuge anywhere, no hole in which to lie?

Strain your hearing!
In repeated gusty surges

Winds are veering,
And their fingers, long and drying,
Strike a music from the bones.
Are these but a dead man's dirges,
Or a living lay that urges
Heart to pity with strange moans?

Everything is held and haunted.

Strain your hearing!
In the byre a cow lows hiding.
Is she haunted
By the same foul nightmare riding
Her with pole-axe, hemp, and cringle,
And a killer's eye and laughter?
Does this eye make her veins tingle
And her throat shake beam and rafter?
Or does she see werwolves halving
Shadows between tree and tree?
Or can it be
She is in the throes of calving?

Surely this is past our knowing.
Ah, to-night we know too well!
We are one, the same breath flowing
Over tongue and tooth and jaw.
Even corpses have a grip on
Sense. We are astray. A bell
Hangs about each neck to draw
Us to herdsman and to shippon.

Outward Bound

1

Pulses in my brain beat anguish.
Is the wall the lock to calm?
Something smoothes me as I languish —
Your proved palm!

Spread out over me for ever
As leaved shadows over sands,
Close beyond the air to sever —
Those two hands!

Setting out you showed, I fingered
Hand-rails meted to my size,
And a leading light has lingered
In your eyes.

Ah, but now you see me slipping
As cell sutures come apart.
Gone! Where did the latest stripping
Lead my heart?

2

But I wake. My stung sense flashes
Out of fibres of coarse stuff,
And I sweep walls clean of ashes.
Hold, enough!

And I wake again that dying —
The enfranchisement of things —
May release my caged blood's flying
Beat of wings.

Heated in that fiery furrow
All these thousand years of doom,
Ancient Styx's waters burrow
In the gloom.

Stench of blood more lye than acid,
Stench of human blood drifts past,
And the hooded night is placid,
And the last.

Windy sails blow out like bladders
As the helmsman's hand appears;
Hempen cords writhe into adders
While he steers.

And I start upon my sailing,
Lips compressed and lids closed tight,
Till my blood's last lamps blur, failing,
Into night.

Highway

How the dusty highway hurries
Over bridge and over stream,
Leaving in forsaken grasses
A white gleam!

Each of the four fellies scurries
As the miller's wagon passes,
One aloft as white as steam,
Hodden bleached from top to toe.

Maple, ash, and linden-tree,
In a row,
Lean as after a carousal,

Ranged there for the wind to tousle
In his early morning glee.

Black-striped mileposts march in order.
On the right, near the wood's border,
Cows are grazing, broad and placid,
Pulling grasses sweet and acid,
Munching, never seen to falter:
Bellied hunger does not slacken.

On the left, near the wood's border,
Cattle feed on quitch and bracken,
Backs like maps that with each quiver
Of the skin will slightly alter;
And each vein looks like a river.

In the dust are tyre-traces,
And these mingle
With horse-droppings and, in places,
Bits of shingle.

Barley-fields stand thick with bristles;
Jets of smoke ascend obliquely;
Stones and thistles
Hedge the crofts that huddle meekly.

Then come marshes downed with heather.

See, a cur as tough as leather,
Each thick ear-flap like a mitten,
Muzzle tarred, coat plucked and bitten,
Barks and leaps about and snuffles.

Fence-grass ruffles,
Showing rags of poppy red.

There a farm-girl sits and shuffles,
Arm in air to beat off flies
From about her neck and head.

Barns of a prodigious size,
Walled with millstones that have trodden
Grain, still swallow
Hay and straw to stuff their hollow
Maws. Did last year's virid leas,
Snapes, and sodden
Fen, and peat-moss flower and teem?

Feathers tumble
As gray wings creak on the breeze.
Then again four cart-wheels rumble.
Over bridge and over stream
How the dusty highway hurries, leaving in forsaken grasses
A white gleam!

*Lady of Porkuni**

On the lake in the manor gardens a light
Still hovers where reeds are ranker,
And a glowing heart floats day and night
Where the lilies lie at anchor.

The light is the lady of Porkuni,
Whose soul is imprisoned in water.
Though her gown and shoes lie peacefully,
There's no rest for the baron's daughter.

* Porkuni, in North-eastern Estonia, or Vironia (Virumaa), lies where the Valge river leaves the lake (*tiik*) in its north-westerly course to Hara creek (*laht*), a minor indentation of the Gulf of Finland. It was the seat of a German manor before the First World War.

And why must she lie in her watery grave
When others have graves that are earthy?
Because love made a willing slave
Of one he had chosen as worthy.

But is there no gale that could blow away
A soul so heavy with sorrow?
Not now that the tale has become a lay
Which yesterday sings to-morrow.

It tells how there once lived in Porkuni keep
A girl without father or mother.
There was no one to guard her innocent sleep
But a restless warrior-brother.

This brother rode out to pillage and burn,
And the girl stayed behind. How quiet
Her life was till winter stood at the turn
And the waters in brooks ran riot!

She left her room again and again
At dawn and when night was falling,
And she felt in her bosom an exquisite pain
When she heard the green spring calling.

In the alder tops a rare bird sang;
Below, a bay ox stood lowing;
Where the ground was still hard and the blue ice rang
Rose a marvel new to her knowing.

She sat by the door in a slender gown,
Her shoes dipped in purple flowers.
Then she rose from her place with a petulant frown
To count the retreating hours.

29

She listened hard with expectant ear,
And her eyes saw creatures together.
"Ah, when will my wandering brother be here?"
She asked as she scanned the weather.

She stood with the question on her pure face,
And her budding breasts were eager.
Her fingers played with some silken lace,
Her knowledge of signs was not meagre.

Will he come by the slopes that were lately snowed?
Will he ride back late or early?
And does that long white ribbon of road
Lead into the hurly-burly?

And out of her milk-stained narrow hand
She teased an insect to flying.
Will he come across that billowy land
Where he rode when the autumn was dying?

The ladybird's wings at last took flight
And stirred her recollection.
"He is coming!" she thought, and the thought took fright.
One came from a strange direction.

Be it true or false that the eagle's wing
Spans skies whether cloudless or laden,
It is truth itself that in early spring
A man's way leads to a maiden.

Her eye was suddenly meshed in his eye,
And hand towards hand was tending.
In the blossoming world these two could descry
A sweetness that seemed unending.

His brow was as proud as her brother's brow,
And he had her brother's graces.
They forgot all else but the here and now
And blent in each other's embraces.

As lips to passionate lips they pressed
In spasms delicious and tender,
The necklace fell from her neck and breast
Into fragments of jewelled splendour.

The summer had swung to its utmost height.
Winter came, and the stream lost motion;
The glass of the lake grew hard and bright,
And the reeds forgot their commotion.

The provident wings of the ladybird
Had failed, or had been deflected;
And the brother who had not written one word
Came back when he was not expected.

When the charger's tramp grew suddenly still,
And she heard a man's feet coming,
The girl grew pale and lost her will,
And her hot heart started drumming.

Already her sweet was souring to smart,
And the floor was strewn with her gladness.
What she had in her heart and under her heart
Was to bring her a mortal sadness.

As he greeted his sister the brother grew curt.
"Why does she blush so and tremble?"
Love, pride, and faith were equally hurt.
"Is she trying now to dissemble?"

"Dear brother, dear brother, have pity on me!
I yielded to true love's pressing.
Now nothing can part us, not even the sea.
Dear brother, give us your blessing."

The brother's hot blood rose on a great shout.
They were in his jurisdiction.
He drew his sword. Thin death flashed out
To lapse in his sister's affliction.

The bounding thud of her lover's head
Hurled horror into her weeping.
Great clusters of berry-red blood were shed;
Some fell in her lap and keeping.

The bold man's anger grew hard and grim;
He had come unscathed from battle.
His sister's eyes could not soften him,
Nor her tearful childish prattle.

A whirlwind raced through boughs without leaves
As he dragged her by her tresses,
The hailstones beat on him down to his greaves,
And the moon bemoaned her distresses.

Through the hard blue ice he hacked a hole,
Then he thrust his sister under.
For a space her body clung to her soul,
But at length death forced them asunder.

Since then on Porkuni Lake a light
Still hovers where reeds are ranker,
And a glowing heart floats day and night
Where the lilies lie at anchor.

Look, the Sea Rises

Look, the sea rises above its level,
Moving through pastures in glittering revel.

Clouds hang about it, and windy flurries;
Foam stains its greenish lips as it hurries.

Everywhere its terrain enlarges;
Timbers are shaken in bridges and barges.

Light flings up from each eye-like eddy;
Nothing can hold the sea now or steady.

Horse-like the waters bound over boulders,
Froth flying over breast and shoulders.

Flashing green hoofs, each wave shows its paces,
Clean as a thoroughbred's and without traces.

Fences down, the sea advances;
Towards your own doorway a stallion prances.

And it pounds holes in your lidded vision,
Neighing with voice of Satanic derision.

Colt

Grass has a barren taste;
Oats are still growing;
In the unbitted mouth
Memories of milk.

Wandering gusts of wind
Play with his beard,
Finger the stubborn
Brush of his copper mane.

Shivers pass over
Harness-shy breast and flank.
Candid between his eyes,
Flashes a blaze.

Round his neck tinkles
Summer sun's song-bell.
In his thews endlessly
Fidgets escape.

Veins taut with anxious blood,
Awkward ears listen
To the sound of
Sledge-hammers striking.

That's not the blacksmith
Or a roused anvil,
And they're not forging
Shoes for those merry legs.

It's not the blacksmith's hand,
But the master's,
Busied in building you
A new abode.

Swollen with sullen heat,
Timbers smell sweetly;
Out of them oozes
Honey-clear gum.

Housed behind board and beam,
You shall know woodlands,
Taste the red clover-tops
At Christmas time.

Then you'll go snowy ways,
Then you'll go wedding ways,
Then you'll go coffin ways,
Little brown colt.

Till then pay heed but to
Dreams in your blood-stream,
Paradise gardens,
Murmurings of God.

Is that the river-horse
Snorting below there,
Where the wet sallows lean?
Or can you see

Barrel-hooped zebras
Rampant in light?
Listen hard, eager-eyed,
Little brown colt.

Orphan

Bent to the sea's commotion,
Out of lost eyes
Stares the gray hovel. Waves' motion
Mingles with seamews' cries.

Home with her lamb she came after
Dark had muffled the hill,

35

Heedless of leering and laughter,
Lips pressed close and still.

There in the evening she lingered,
Eyes wet with old despair.
Thorns seemed to shoot as she fingered
Harvests of russet hair.

Was that the swift's throat calling
To her where shadows rolled?
Serpentine moonbeams falling
Twisted her torques of gold.

Bent to the sea's commotion,
Out of lost eyes
Stares the gray hovel. Wave's motion
Mingles with tears and sighs.

All Over Again

Your ways again are stonier in their feel,
And you have forfeited long love's correction.
Tempests have roused the winds to insurrection.
You tramp the flats and slopes with dragging heel.
Your lodestar shines within. You even steal
Your fingers from the guiding palm's direction.
Then, all at once, your vision and reflection
Grow clear as water and, like ice, congeal.

And now you burn. Your breath is like an oast;
Your spirit's only purpose to refashion
Itself in an inexorable passion.
Ice grows below, a new god on its post.

But once, illuminated, you may wonder
Whether you have not made the selfsame blunder.

St. George

When the mailed victor's lance had pinned the dire
Beast, and its fangs and claws gave up the fight,
His loosened hair blossomed in aureoled light
That made a shadow of his victim's fire;
His smiling lips were just seen to suspire;
His shoulders put forth wings of bannered might.
This was his triumph's most exalted height:
He could have died, caught in his wings' high gyre.

But champions are scarce. Who has not striven
To combat the malignant and insane
And, missing their Achilles' heel, been driven
To coddle wickedness with words that sain,
With tender names that should not have been spoken,
Only to find its strength and rage unbroken?

Remembrance and Pledge

Now let us stand with bowed and naked head,
Remembering what is left and what is dead.

All we have lost and death's dividing wall —
These give us strength that nothing can appal.

Our homeland's wrongs shall make our patience bold:
Let us defend her wall-like, young and old.

37

Love of the earth passes from heart to heart,
Earth of our dead, in which we each have part.

Much else has perished, yet these are not dead —
Our pride and rage: let's stand with lifted head.

Kassari Cemetery

The chapel by the long untrodden
Seashore comes up to meet my leisure
And love. The crosses stand, some sodden
And half-submerged at the sea's pleasure.

That rugged cross is lichened, hoary,
And buried deep in bush and flower.
It is the one. Some of our story
Is there to read this sunset hour.

I just make out upon the cross's
Rough weathered face the still abiding
Names of my people. But their glosses
Are nothing to those white and gliding

Boats. There are houses too — none warmer
Than my loved haunts . . . But they have vanished.
For all these things were matched with former
Times. Now even birds are dead or banished.

GUSTAV SUITS

My Island

Still I keep sailing and sailing,
And seeking an isle in the sea:
I have sought it long already
Where the random winds sail free.

The sea has many islands
And havens expectant with light,
But I cannot find the island
I dreamed in the dazzled night.

And still my vessel keeps scudding
On a swaying circular plain,
And the clouds above me go swaying,
And I seek my island in vain.

Autumn Song

Skies are fading, the fields lie bare,
And the rank rains have crowded the air.

Landscapes drown as the drops condense,
Sickening the heart with blurring sense.

O that the skirts of the rain were lifted!
O that the mists were husked and sifted!

But the motionless air turns gray
As the mists suck the dregs of day.

Shadows muffle the wayfarer's goal;
Soon the night will be blind to the pole.

O for the eye of a star to the friendless!
O that the darkness did not seem endless!

Nebulosa

Delirium and dreams had left dark traces;
October dribbled from the boughs in rain;
We wandered, prisoners to subtle pain,
In desolate and autumn-littered places.
Dusk muffled the bleak stone of built-up spaces;
At corners saffron lamps spilt pool and stain;
We wandered, prisoners to subtle pain,
In desolate and autumn-littered places.

Beyond last reach the gardens of delight,
And hope of miracles scaled from the sight,
Love fled into the darkness and the city.
And without dreams now at the turn of tide,
We walked at random, mute and side by side,
Till flagging limbs had drained the heart of pity.

Modern Fairy-Tale

Now the way cuts through the whiteness
Under heavens drained of brightness.

What are those thrust out of night?
Crofts along the forest edges,
Homes approached by steel of sledges
Rest after the march of light.

All at once a gust of wind
Brings shrill cries and lamentations,
And the shadows leave their stations,
And a fear falls on the mind.

Whose that sighing? Whose that wail,
Fading, fainting, swelling, nearing,
As its echoes seek a hearing
For a modern fairy-tale?

Listening heart is torn by doubt.
Something stabs to bone and marrow;
Someone utters screams that harrow;
Someone suddenly laughs out.

Do not stand there over long.
It is all a hideous story.
You are in it, and the hoary
Roof is home, where you belong.

Now the way cuts through the whiteness
Under heavens drained of brightness.

To a Child

Your laughing voice broke in upon my quiet,
Your laughing voice;
My thoughts and dreams and studies mixed in riot
At your light choice.

Hair like ripe leaves and, in the cheeks, twin hollows;
Hair like ripe leaves,
And shining eyes as swift as summer swallows
About the eaves.

Of life and light your being is compounded,
Of life and light;
For days this house has joyously resounded
With your delight.

Sweet April bud, may coming tempests spare you,
Sweet April bud;
And do not press me hard: I would not snare you
With troubled blood.

Your happy feet, ah, may they dance for ever,
Your happy feet,
And follow ways where clouds and shadows sever
And sunbeams meet.

What heavy souls have seasoned grief with laughter,
What heavy souls
Have stood and whistled, eyes on the hereafter,
Where Lethe rolls?

Criss-cross

I paid no heed to thunder;
My ways have gone asunder;
And did I gain or blunder?
And am I strong or weak?

I have known wind and weather,
I have torn every tether,
And, as a bird its feather,
Have shown my colours plain.

Did you not hear me singing;
Blood in my temples dinging;
The pole and canvas swinging?
Which of us holds the field?

I move through spring desires
As the brief dawn expires;
But shall I kindle fires?
Am I a flame or smoke?

So with time's strains and stresses
One changes course or presses,
And the detached eye guesses:
A mask to straiten truth?

Passing Bell

There is a silence in the village
As of the mists upon the hill:
The chapel road winds out of tillage
Through sultry heath to cool and still.

Listen: the passing bell is ringing.
I stop awhile and hold my breath.
It seems as if a soul were winging
Out of the chrysalis of death.

"How strange the things beyond possession
Of mind!" I thought and went my way.
"There goes a funeral procession;
Here laughing children run at play."

"How strange the things beyond expression
Of heart!" I pondered on my way.
"Death moves there in a dark procession;
I walk alone with life and day."

Once in the winter through a smother
Of snow the passing bell was tolled:
It was the memory of my mother
The clangour bore to heath and wold.

I came and saw her body lying
Rigid upon the rigid deal:
She had already done with dying,
And death had sealed her with his seal.

Her lips were closed on pain and sorrow;
Her long disease had left no trace;
White silence filled her white to-morrow;
And tranquil pride lay on her face.

Listen: the passing bell is ringing.
I stop awhile and hold my breath.
It seems as if a soul were winging
Out of the chrysalis of death.

Those hands had tended grain and weeded;
That back had lifted yoke and pails;
The cows and dogs loved her as she did
Them. Is it but son's love that fails?

Her son, released from school and science,
Came rarely to recall her eyes:
He followed winds and clouds. Defiance
Refused to know her wisdom wise.

Ah, what a miracle the power
Of mother's love to last and save!
And what despair was in the hour
That brought me to this alien grave!

Once in the winter through a smother
Of snow the passing bell was tolled:
It was the memory of my mother
The clangour bore to heath and wold.

Over her now the sharp sweet-briar
Flowers aloof among the trees.
My ways once led from high to higher,
And they have led to this and these.

Some day, tall bell, you will be ringing
Again, and one will hold his breath.
Some day, tall bell, you will be ringing
The darkness of another death.

Pools in the Swamp

The surface of the swamp holds pools unnumbered.
Can it be rusty water that lies tongueless and still,
Or mindless pain staring with mute eyes that numb the will?

45

The surface of the swamp holds pools unnumbered.

Slow silver bubbles globe upon the water.
O yearnings, secret wishes, that hide in the swamp's night!
O dreams that blot out suddenly, failing in mid-flight!

Slow silver bubbles globe upon the water.

Clawed to the earth, the stunted birches cower.
The treacherous virid floor of the swamp hollows and quakes
To straying feet, and the turbid glass of the water breaks.

Clawed to the earth, the stunted birches cower.

The live swamp teems with myriads of midges.
They fill the eyes and nostrils, and suck blood from the vein,
And choke desire, and creep in the heart, and daze the brain.

The live swamp teems with myriads of midges.

Nightfall over the Meadow

Still glossed with the zenith glow of day,
The sun's last spears surrender,
And now, as the dyed world ebbs away,
The chosen inherit their splendour.

As whispers awake on the chastened earth,
These pass to the champaigns of glory,
Where suns are untarnished by death and birth,
And care has no tongue in story.

But into oblivion such shall fall
As barter in shames and rages,

And lapsed into darkness, beyond recall,
Shall languish through desolate ages.

So vision sees open the valves of light,
Sees evil's defeated traces,
And, in the pure depths of the summer night,
The justice of starry spaces.

Far Cuckoos

Shadows and you waiting breathlessly
Listened to far cuckoos call.
Through the long gardens moved deathlessly
Dreams that each spring shall recall.

Silences studied in wondering
Listened to far cuckoos call.
Airs without words floated sundering
Dreams that each spring shall recall.

Strings breaking pattern in mutiny
Listened to far cuckoos call,
And the dreams faded to scrutiny —
Dreams that each spring shall recall.

Scarlet Dawning

Is that the dye of the sun's plumage flaring
Along the trees, or cut-throat's lantern glaring?
No cock shrills here. The breeching of a gun
Snaps to. There is no time to love the sun.

47

Not of dawn's scarlet only the new fire
Kindles in woods. O ambushed robber band!
O armed collision with imperial ire!
The scarlet quickens through the passive land.

Dawn, did you ever greet in the white weather
So many forest brothers* leagued together?

Ringed Moon

Moonlight falls distant and dry,
Frosting the snowfields in lustre;
Trees shudder darkly and sigh;
And, to win warmth, seem to cluster
Where the dog howls to the sky.

> Life has locked and barred her portals
> On the death-skis of immortals.

Moonlight falls distant and dry,
Silvering the homesteads to sadness;
Trees shudder darkly and sigh;
Cares of the world and its madness
Rise with the howls to the sky.

> Life has locked and barred her portals
> On the death-skis of immortals.

Moonlight falls distant and dry;
Ice-blinded window-panes glisten;
Trees shudder darkly and sigh.
Why do you strain so to listen
When the dog howls to the sky?

* The literal meaning of *metsavennad* "guerillas, partisans."

Life has locked and barred her portals
On the death-skis of immortals.

The Circle Is Not Sealed

Sing, fancy, of that dream,
The white and graceful figure;
Song, of youth's mood and vigour,
For sense can now but guess
What longing came with press
Of stars, with scent and fashion
Of leaves, with vernal passion.
As winds to shadows seem,
Sing, fancy, of far dream.

The nights had cancelled sleep,
Head coolness, spirit gladness,
And sense was near to madness.
Light, springtime, and slim grace
Walked in a flowering space;
Desire from sharp grew tender,
Then stayed before surrender.
Now mind and hours reap;
The nights have banished sleep.

Sad chords struck on the keys
By pure and pliant fingers;
The touching air still lingers.
Song of black butterfly,
How this could have told why
My tongue seemed to grow rigid,
My sense aloof and frigid!
Yet my heart pined with these
Frail chords struck on the keys.

A goatsucker whirred low,
Black in the night's pale clearing.
A dismal sound or cheering?
Blossom fell by the road;
Moonlight and water flowed;
Our ways had fused together
Under spring leaf and feather;
The cricket scraped his bow;
The dusky birds sang low.

Has the clear wine of moon
And stars a bitter savour?
When autumn nights grow graver
Does love's sharp casement light
Sting with unused delight?
Do eyes turn moist with sorrow
When blind panes face to-morrow?
Do you still read in moon
And stars a poignant rune?

The circle is not sealed
To the requickening powers.
It seemed as if but hours
Had passed. How strange the fears
That once had called them years!
For as the stars grow livid,
The vision blossoms vivid
That soul to soul revealed:
The circle is not sealed.

Vicious Circle

Topsy-turvy things came dogging
Hate. The flogger got a flogging,

Executioners were strangled,
And the violator dangled.
Lynch-law fumed and raged and howled,
Talon-fisted, iron-jowled,
There was jangling, there was wrangling:
Over fields and over fallows
Lead the butchers to the gallows!

Evil was not battened under,
Nor did passions stint their thunder.

Topsy-turvy days came dogging
Death. The rebels got a flogging;
Vengeance whimpered in a mesh;
Pits were dug and crammed with flesh;
Serpent seed was soon forgotten
With the worms that ploughed it rotten.
There was prying, there was spying:
Rear a gallows for the killers,
Spill the blood of the blood-spillers!

Evil was not battened under,
Nor did passions stint their thunder.

Then up spoke a shrewd coeval:
"Both these turns were bred from evil.
Off with scales that seal the pupils,
Blinding men to mind and scruples!
Comfortless as pedant schooling
Is revenge's iron ruling.
Only when love's lips have spoken
Shall we see the circle broken."

Abandoned Manor

His narrow duty done, the sentry paces
Out of his world, then stiffens like a rod.
A chalk-white and palatial manor faces
Autumn across stripped bough and leaf-strewn sod.
Messengers crowd the door. His absent Grace's
Art treasures lie there rifled. Word or nod
From that damp raincoat rules the secret places
Where once the major-domo was a god.

Among the scattered things a lovely vision,
Canova's Venus, stands in dazzling stone,
With calm eyes fixed beyond the crude derision
Of harrowing times, immortal, and alone.
And though her gracious hand has lost the fingers
That held the golden bowl, the sweet smile lingers.

Six Candles

Tempests have shaken the house of the years.
Little heart's treasure has straightened and grown.
Bravely the light of six candles appears.

These are the symbols of laughter and tears,
Glimmering sixfold, rehearsing the known.
Tempests have shaken the house of the years.

What exultations, what cavernous fears
Walked with the sower, his heart in the sown!
Bravely the light of six candles appears.

As out of weels among rushes she peers

With those big eyes, self-secure and alone.
Tempests have shaken the house of the years.

Bravely the light of six candles appears.

Sympathy

No cloudless sun was ever so appealing
As is the beam that struggles to be free
Against the wind and rain across the reeling
Skies and holds sight as by divine decree.
The tempest's rage can never master feeling
As does the twisted pine-top's agony,
Its semipendent branches still revealing
The gale's path where the shore invades the sea.

Whatever has been persecuted, harried,
Tortured, and buried by this world is carried
Into the generous heart, for this grows tender
In face of facts, decisive as time's dial,
Of striving pitched against the storms of trial,
The will to live that cannot know surrender.

Warning to a Workman

Brother, let the bridle
Curb the words you say
As you kick the idle
Cork that bars your way.

Turn your hearing, brother,
From seditious speech

As you reel home, smother
What the slums would teach.

Keep your head, remember,
Staggering up the back,
Forests and November
Hid what bleeding wrack.

In a Time of Arrests

Lilac clusters, hanging over walled-in gardens,
Breathe a drowsy influence that burdens
Hearts these summer evenings prone to error,
Which inherit spring's unwonted terror.
Don't ask green-capped men the way or whether
To proceed in file or all together.
To the north-west you discern a glowing
Streak, and all around are people going
Criss-cross ways, their homes without protection,
Eyes blind to the light's pale resurrection.
There is fear about that you may vanish
From your home, a fear no words shall banish.
So you have no time to speak with tested
Friendships. Who knows? — you might be arrested.
"Such nights bring the Promised Land much nearer.
Get into the wall-paper," the jeerer
Jeers. The tongue breaks loose from its frustration
Only on discreet investigation.
Listen to the nightingale: those tender
Notes may give you sleep before surrender,
But the cattle-truck with lock and grating
Looms behind the curtained window, waiting.

Word

No good can ever come to such as spend
Their minds and days in futile brooding on
Ruins. What are you since what seemed the end?
Someone from somewhere still. You have your burden.

Your brain, a grave of embers that shall smoulder,
Acknowledges no despot as its master.
You never raise your hand above your shoulder
To greet. Your words are close since the disaster.

Words live from mouth to mouth, are never lonely,
And find even in ash an inspiration:
So, without ebbing to dumb heartbeats only,
My words, grow wings, rise, fly to every nation.

Homeless

You have known days. You have seen ways.
Not without shelter you lived there,
Not without a home of your own:
There was then a room, a refuge
From wild winds, a house to house you.

Sinister times have settled on us,
Times of trial and bitterness.
Ceilings snapped and slumped in showers;
Stacks came hurtling down like hailstones;
Fiery floors crackled viciously;
Hearts are smouldering even here.

True, the gales have tousled your hair,
But the heat was never hotter
Since you yourself became homeless.

55

Jaan Oks

Without Trace

I must completely escape from my kind,
Leaving no ultimate trace behind,
Past the sheer heavens and over the mountains
Into oblivion's occident fountains.
O for the sceptre to govern there
Aeons of time in the empires of air!
It is a glorious thing to go friendless,
Lost in expanses whose frontiers are endless.

One thing is clear beyond rumour of doubt:
All trace of me must be blotted out!
And I shall sever the bonds that have bound me,
Break through the spiders' webs around me.

As I Gaze Towards Ashen Arches

As I gaze towards ashen arches
Past the tall and rigid trees,
I can see a grin that starches
Lips, a nakedness of knees.
In my eyes are tips of flowers,
Black seed wedded to the earth,
Forests built by virid showers,
Madness in the throes of birth.

Stretch the Catgut over Sorrow

Stretch the catgut over sorrow;
Take a rush-bow from the brake.
Here are voices from the barrow
Come on gusts that stab and shake.
Why, my heart, this fevered beating?
Why is that rock assailed by rage?
What far song is that bird cheeping?
What is that beast at in its cage?

V̲ILLEM RIDALA*

Intuition of Spring

Something is flashing and flickering and flying
Towards where the hillsides are hazy;
And where the woodlands are mazy
Something is calling and clamouring and crying.

Skies swept with splendour are vying in laughter
With the ground's glittering grasses;
And the light wind, as it passes,
Draws the soft shadow-feet pittering after.

Something is flashing and flickering and flying
Towards where the hillsides are hazy;
And where the woodlands are mazy
Something is calling and clamouring and crying.

Deep in the heart an invisible finger
Touches a string full of sweetness,

* Pseudonym of Villem Grünthal.

Something takes refuge in fleetness —
Something whose echoings lovingly linger.

At Daybreak

Into the new light of skies beginning to pale,
High above the dappled grass of rise and vale,
Through the billowing gauze of mists that lift and trail,
Star fades after star.

And across the languor of the summer dawn,
Lying silent-lipped on acre, wood, and lawn,
Faltering sounds of life, like footsteps of a fawn,
Rustle dim and far.

On a Dun

Out of vaporous mists hemming in the beaches,
Like a glowing vein, vivid in the grayness,
Shines the narrow strait mirroring the distant
Light of the evening.

From the heavy north all along the skyline,
Jagged and blue-black, poised on empty waters,
Lifts a line of woods binding spells of evil
Out of the shadows.

Terror grips the heart as the deep unconscious
Mind revolves the known, days that time has taken,
Days when dauntless hearts, pierced by hostile lances,
Mingled with darkness,

And when iron death walked through smoky hazes,
Stalked with cross in hand over corpse and rampart,
When — soil drenched with blood — dwindling suns of freedom
Rolled to their setting.

Winter Evening

Over luminous snow-violet meadows,
 Patterned with vacillant shadows,
Fall the flames of sunset metals,
 Red as rose petals.

Over frigid illimitable spaces,
 Smooth and bare, passes
  A lonely road,
   Crossing a lode
Where clumps of rimed willows
Lean over glazed shallows.

Hugging the road's flanged bed,
 Sled follows sled
  Towards pale lunar glories,
   Where night's door is,
    Far away.

Wild Geese

Necks straight as rods and their webbed feet flexed under them,
 reddish and rigid,
Fiery glints in their eyes, left by the embers of light,
Palely they swim in the cavernous blue of the night's solemn
 spaces

60

Down the long channel of day, ranged in a transient line.
Now and again with the powerful upthrust of wings lifts a
     clamour,
Resonant, minor, and harsh under the dome of the sky:
Bird calls to following bird in a throaty appeal as it passes
On its uncharted smooth way, locked in the corporate flight.
Far at their feet now the beaches and forests are flooded with
     darkness,
Only the shadow-streaked wave glints with a dull meagre hue
Where the decaying light's steadily vanishing yellowish glimmer
Walks on the face of the sea, clouded to breath-misted glass.
Over the heads of the geese, see, the ranked constellations march
     forward,
Filming wide spaces with gauze, strewing the sky with thin flames.
Blue-black and lonely, the sails of the clouds belly out on a voyage
Towards the lost ports of the light, steered by a freshening wind.
Bound to their shadows that glide on the edge of the clouds'
     rounded canvas,
Move the close ranks of the geese under the dusk and the stars,
And as they move, their long voices scale flights of the glittering
     stairway
Leading to ultimate peace, whence humbled echoes descend.
Nothing can stay the wild geese on their journey towards sultrier
     waters,
Not even sea-circled plains, meadows of long-furrowed grass,
Where they alighted but yesterday, welcomed by moisture and
     umbrage,
Weary with hours of flight, longing for beak-to-wing rest.
Forward the voyagers swing in the gathering candour of starlight,
Lingering coals in their eyes, breasts filled with breath of the
     night.
See, as they stretch out their necks once again into distance and
     dwindling,
Light limns the line of their ebb, colours with relics of day.

Then they all fade one by one, strung in file, into mufflings of
     twilight,
Beaks growing mute as their wings, voices delivered to time.
Only the lonely black clouds left behind on the sky-sea continue
On their slow voyage through space under the star-spangled
     night.
And, far below, the tall lighthouses beat the near air with their
     lashes,
Wealing the night-conquered sea, stippled with pearls from the
     Way.

*Epitaphium**

Life's is the lease of a season; deeds of pure courage outlast it,
Loyal with love of one's land — love that goes silent to death.
Valiant remembrance is dateless and burns like a flame on the
     darkness.
See, out of destiny's night lifts the far torch of renown.

---

* The third line, in Finnish and Swedish translation, is inscribed on a monument
in Helsinki, commemorating the supreme sacrifice of the Finnish volunteers who
fell in the Estonian war of independence.

ARTUR ADSON

You Hold My Heart with Hallowed Power

You hold my heart with hallowed power
That seals my ardour one with duty,
And you have taught me not to cower
Before the mystery of your beauty.

Out of blank lanes of tortuous passion
I came into your sudden glory;
And loving eyes foretold compassion,
And love annulled a sombre story.

Your seeing blood moves through my blindness,
Disclosing heavens beyond to-morrow,
And on my face the loving kindness
Of fingers intimate with sorrow.

It is so strange that this was granted
To me, the earthiest of the earthy!
I walk the world as if enchanted
And dream that love has made me worthy.

Once Again I Journeyed towards You

Once again I journeyed towards you
Over hursts and sanded valleys,
Sped by dreams and windy sallies.
Once again I journeyed towards you.

How I yearned to see that marvel
Walking white as Heaven's daughter,
Bearing gifts to bird and water!
How I yearned to see that marvel!

And to sit before the Virgin,
Hold her feet in loving duty,
Watch her eyes' excelling beauty;
And to sit before the Virgin.

Once again I journeyed towards you,
And I clasped you but in fancy,
Kissed you only in my fancy.
Once again I journeyed towards you.

God's Children

See, how they bundle them into cramped spaces,
Leaving each waiting behind a bolted door,
Paying no heed to words that implore,
Laughing contemptuously into boarded faces.

And how they load them with daily distresses,
Who have aspired to touch the days with glamour,
Take away the weariness from shovel and hammer —
Beings that were born to receive caresses.

64

And how they wound them with coarse behaviour,
Beings whose lips are pure with virtuous loving,
Beings whose eyes are gentle and moving,
Whose gracious lives are as speech with their Saviour.

Give that one his wish who patiently burrows,
Filling his coffers with niggardly treasure.
They — the despised — have longings past measure;
They are God's children and drive his straight furrows.

Workdays

Workdays plod unkempt in single
File to dead issues,
And the fibres of living mingle
Into harsh tissues.

They are blotted now, all those early
Days and their glitter.
What is left to us here seems merely
Weather-stained litter.

Skies hang desolate-hued and bellied
Over pinched vision;
Feet have grown like a naked-fellied
Wheel's indecision.

Work will never assort with pleasure
If it is tainted
With a despair that leaves shrunk leisure
Dull and unsainted.

Workdays rally to six in number —
Some reckon seven —

And they plod on even in slumber,
Outlawed from heaven.

I have never raised voice for riches,
But myself only.
Given besides roof, bread, and flitches,
Could joy feel lonely?

Nor do I crave these gifts in plenty.
If water plashes
Over stones as when I was twenty,
Will mouth taste ashes?

Aspen, Aspen, Why This Quivering?

Aspen, aspen, why this quivering?
Birch, how changed your new tale's colouring?

Quiverings sort with a red story;
Autumn tales are coloured yellow.

The red story tells of sorrow,
The yellow tale of coming death.

Of whose sorrow? — Brother's sorrow,
Sister's sorrow, comrade's sorrow.

Every home has its grief of dying,
Every stalk must perish sometime.

Branches fail in sap and vigour,
Lifting bone-like towards the heavens.

But in their dry desolation
Roosting winds still fashion a dwelling.

Winds inside them, winds around them,
Winds above them, winds beneath them

Ply and snap the brittle aspens,
Shake and bend the pliant birches.

Where shall they go, the forest rangers?
Where will the hare win back his heart?

Who will give shelter to the songsters,
Leaves to hide the silent bird?

Aspen quivering in the cold,
Birch-tree of the yellowing tale,

We are one in the same sorrow,
Waiting silently for death.

See, the sun withdraws in prayer,
Clouds range in a funeral throng.

It is raining to exhaustion,
Even wires drip with tears.

Ailing

Did eager laughter ever brim your heart?
You can't recall; I can't recall.
Care's trap has swallowed joy into its smart.
No trace at all of joy — at all!

And could you once with flying manes have bowled
Along the way, the primrose way?
So that at bends sparks leapt as axle rolled —
And rolls away, beyond to-day.

New suns no longer bring the old delight.
Blossom is blown, the scents forblown.
Day treads on day with intervals of night
Towards the unknown, the gray unknown.

I lift your sorrowing hand on to my knees.
It is so ill, so very still.
And as I prop you into pillowed ease,
You stay so still, you have no will.

Your faded lips are closed to common speech
With a dark seal, a cruel seal;
Your song-wood is cut down and out of reach
Of sowing hands' and spring's appeal.

But who sows woods that singing birds may rest
In the close foliage of a tree?
There is no place in which a bird may nest
That I can see, can ever see.

Through Dreams

Something hinders me from sleeping
With an airy plaintive cheeping:
Water-bird and singing throstle
Beat the glass with urgent jostle.

Their thin notes are sad and lowly
Like a music frail and holy.
They are going far to-morrow,
And the garden droops in sorrow.

Something breaks my threefold quiet
With a rush of muffled riot:

Gusts of wind the gales have shaken
Call me loudly to awaken.

Their swift feet are full of flurry,
And their mouths are hot with hurry:
They will scatter like the thunder
When the dark is wrenched asunder.

Something hinders me from sleeping
With a tense and lidless peeping:
High in heaven a star is gleaming,
And its light comes steeply streaming.

But the light is without gladness,
And it stales my heart with sadness . . .
In the coppice and the heather
Hiss the drops of changing weather.

Who Walks . . . ?

Who walks familiar ways that I walked there?
Who stops to let his seeing eyes go winging,
To listen to the bells of comfort ringing,
To stroke the corn-ears as he shapes a prayer?

Who then turns homewards with that Sunday look,
Enters his home, back turned to barn and byre,
And sees his mother building up the fire,
His father at the table with the Book?

Whom do the children greet with shrilling cries,
Pushing their bud-like heads into the burly,
Yet tender hands that smooth their flaxen curly
Hair, and who looks down into dancing eyes?

69

None walks the highway churchwards any more;
The house and outhouses are wood for burning;
For many souls there can be no returning;
And corn is choked with weeds unknown before.

HENRIK VISNAPUU

Out of Those Withered Memories

Out of those withered memories
Intoxicating perfume flows —
Jasmine, bird-cherry, lilac, guelder-rose;
Out of long withered memories.

My wakened senses swoon under the spell
Of an apocalypse of happiness —
Of blossoms, winnowed light, and her caress;
My senses swoon under their triple spell.

And these recall the spent delight:
Jasmine, bird-cherry, lilac, rose,
Light, and her body's white repose;
All these recall the spent delight.

Do Not Destroy Man!

I am held in derision;
For while I was asleep they were killing a man;

As I drew the clothes over me they were hanging a man,
They were blinding heart and vision.

I am held in derision.
How can I lie down to sleep forgetting that man;
Knowing, as I know, that they were hanging a man,
That they were blinding vision!

Stung by the poet's burning vision,
I want to cry aloud: Do not destroy man!
I want to cry incessantly: Help to preserve man!
I am held in derision.

Through this deed of derision
How deeply I am humbled, for you have killed a man.
How can I feel one with you when you kill a man,
When you blind heart and vision?

I am held in derision.
How can I bring myself to say: Destroy man?
How can I justify you when you destroy man,
When you blind heart and vision?

By foul cruelty that numbs vision
You have been betrayed into killing a man.
I know with my blood that man must not kill man.
I am held in derision.

Christmas Eve

Stars glittered in the sky. The moon was lost.
By the roadside the trees were furred with frost.
It was cold. It was peaceful. It was evening.

72

Sledges drove to church in air that was still.
Mine was mounting a bypath up a hill.
It was Christmas. It was Saturday. It was evening.

When I reached the summit I saw a light.
Where the snow had melted, the earth yawned black as night.
It was cold. There was fire. It was evening.

The fire burned crackling. I lingered on the crest.
A new-born child slept at its mother's breast.
It was peaceful. It was Christmas. It was evening.

I marvelled and stood silent in the fire's gleam.
What I saw I thought was magic or a dream.
It was horrible. It was cold. It was evening.

The mother's lips murmured in a mournful tone:
"My boy sleeps. I am without shelter and alone."
A star glittered over her head. It was evening.

And I bent over her head and touched her hand.
The trees were clothed in silver, like the land.
She was an outcast. It was Christmas. It was evening.

This Evening

Everything is strangely still around me,
As if death's jaws were nearing for the kill,
And I the quarry? Oh, what edge could kill
This ponderous gray silence that seems to impound me?
I am all but exhausted; Ing is going to die,
And my soul is blind with blindness beyond the eye.

It was only last night. Or had the morning
Light sent feelers out to where lands lay dim?

I was immersed in sleep. Ah, sleep could dim
My agonies, settling without wing of warning.
Wherever Ing beckoned, the loved, the beautiful,
I followed with child's feet, loving and dutiful.

And then I stood again in Narva city,*
In that stone solitude of towering walls.
Not first or last their massive horror walls
Me in. Laughter meanwhile had been quenched by pity.
Who was he that did not sell me a black shirt in my dream?
And he who kept back from me the plunging resonant stream?

Why is everything so hushed around me,
As if very death were ambushed for the kill,
And I the victim? What weapon could kill
This dense malignant silence that seems to impound me?
I am all but exhausted; Ing is going to die,
And my soul is blind with blindness beyond the eye.

Death

When he potters round the weathered bigging,
Groans in timbers, sets the floor-boards creaking,
Rattles latch and door and leaves the hinges squeaking,
Heavy loss is written in his begging.
Why did this plant blossom at day's barren ending,
Putting forth its rosy cross-shaped flower?
Now my sleep is wholly beyond mending;
I have lain here staring hour after hour.

* An enormous stronghold overlooking the turbulent river of the same name in
Vironia (Virumaa) and facing the fortress of Jaanilinna (Ivangorod), founded by
the Russian tsar, Ivan III, in 1492.

What is it that surges out of stubble
On to highway with a noise of clopping?
Father is in earth; the colt fast in the stable;
Nothing, surely, but the well-beam chopping.
That is straw upon a hidden shoulder.
See, it thrusts out like a boar's wide bristles.
Someone stumbles darkly on a boulder,
And in winnowing-fans the night-wind whistles.

Listen, that's a hoof upon the paving,
Without iron, a hoof that signals danger;
In its retinue runs many a loyal cur.
Oh, this sweat, this fear at the heart's core!
Hopeful suddenly, we say a passing stranger,
For we know to put him up to-night would mean disaster.
Then my mother weeps, and I am out of breath
With anxiety. There is no braving
What's to come: the house is without master.

It is death; the stranger's name is death.

On Easter Night

As if Mary's feet had walked on heaven's mould,
Bracken, brilliant and unique, has put out flowers,
And space blossoms like a garden nursed through cold.
Those are vernal constellations.
Pour into my heart the power
Of renewal, Spring, awake in saps above.

Heaven's foliage waves how solemn and how high!
And its myriad petals flutter veering.
Light breeds wings and stirs the heart to cry:
This is spring come with his luminous hands!

75

Furl me, Spring, into a clearness,
Still and lucent, with the soul of her I love.

I have come from wintry landscapes lost to day;
Snow has smoothed my footprints with its pallor.
Jesus sits here by a ditch, holding a spray,
Round his hair a saintly colour.
Spring, with clement hand, release my hope's imprisoned dove.

False God of All Animate Things

I am filled with utter misgiving,
O Idol of all animate things;
It was you who gave me to the living
And endued my fancy with wings.

A fire has marshalled its forces
To annex the subsolar world,
And the tramp of starry horses
And their neighing are massively hurled
Over space. What escape with wings furled?
Heart, deeper into bogs and mosses!

Oh, I am racked with misgiving,
False God of all animate things.
It was you made me sort with the living.
Release me from time and its stings.

Serpent tongues flicker from the shingle;
Trees, horned like bullocks, toss;
A giant moon, as red as an ingle,
Weights my brain with loss;
And a burning gravel is blown across
My mouth, and my teeth meet in bell-like jingle.

O Idol of idols,
O life most holy,
O burning heels of god-like derision,
Along what ways am I being carried?
You scorch the air with fire,
Pour blood into my vision.
I feel life's tonnage and tire;
Raining sand has made my mouth arid.
At the feet of the Idol how lowly!

False God of all creation,
And its matted source and fountain,
I look from my days' mountain:
We slowly journey
In the wake of your conflagration.

Rain

Millions of sunken eyes,
Millions of lips like leather,
Thrust from the desolate earth,
Wait for the end of dearth,
Wait for new-coloured skies,
Yearn for the rainy weather.

Bless the speared things that grow,
Lowly that pushes towards higher,
Seed in the nursing clay.
Staked by horizons of day,
Lies the tiller's lean hope
Under enduring fire.

Bless and prosper the rain,
Rifts in the lofty sluices.

Break the dry witchcraft of rest;
Turn the heeled pressure of rust
From the potential grain;
Reconcile hope and its uses.

Rustling and hissing start —
Growth and moisture are wedded —
Over marsh, acre, and lea.
Pent up forces burst free;
Rain streaks the air like yarn;
Men stand about bare-headed.

Thanks for the overturned tun,
Thanks for the hurtling showers,
Thanks for the swollen stream.
Eyes of the ploughlands gleam,
Washed by the rain and the sun
In that transfiguring hour.

Eel

But sting my heart and I take to flight . . .
You rise like a serpent out of the night
And wind about me in spasms.
Did one see my eyes burning in that lost hour:
I know I am prey to a murderous power,
As that evil is sprung from a chasm.

Cold tears descend from the heavy leaves.
My mouth is acrid, my spirit grieves.
Ah, swallow this bitter anguish.
My heart's red vats are still unsated,
And they have slowly accumulated
The slimes in which serpents languish.

Like an eel out of midnight pools you emerge,
And my spirit is seized by a shuddering surge,
Yet my hands do not feel a revulsion.
Where is your habitat? Where your beginning,
Where are the hidden haunts of your sinning?
The depths of lascivious convulsion?

What thirst for your tiny mouth my lips feel!
Your body is boneless, like that of an eel,
And painted black, gold, and livid.
I thrill at the sight of your fierce surrender;
Your touch is destructive, yet strangely tender,
Your eyes are hypnotic and vivid.

My God, I am kneeling down in the grass! ...
As a girl you are brittle and cutting as glass,
As a woman — a vampire vision.
I dread your stung passion's secret places,
Yet I follow your swift irresistible graces,
And accept the final derision.

Flame and White Sand

Flame and white sand
On the heavens:
Grief and its leaven
Merge to disband.

Brilliant far world,
To what beaches,
Avidly reaching,
Is the eye hurled?

79

I'm of the doomed;
You shall linger.
But how much longer
When stars have gloomed?

Out of earth's night
In brief motion
Visions and notions
Strain towards the light.

Doored eternity
Does not move me,
Nor madness proving
Infinity.

Conjuration

Mindless, like the many
Drunk with love's sweet name,
I am old as any
Resurrected flame.

Rise in new-found beauty,
Ing and those dear lips,
Save me from cold duty
To my soul's eclipse.

It is time you listened
To my pleading voice:
Twisted griefs have christened
Poetry to their choice.

Rise again immortal,
Ing, my Virginland,

Save us all from mortal
Blood-lust and red hand.

Kaleva Clans*

Eastern fury stirs and smoulders
Till it bursts in conflagration.
Ancient Kalevala's holders,
Here are words of consecration:
"Winning back the lost transition
Lands shall be our sacred mission."

Where are Ilmarine's forges?
Are his limbs still firmly rooted?
See, the avid steppe disgorges
Thieves. Is Sampo to be looted?
Ladoga and Peipus-water
Teem with Tooni's birds of slaughter.

Somian peoples, how much longer
Will you yield to witch and wizard,
Letting hostile hopes grow stronger,
Filling Baba Yaga's gizzard?
Winning back the lost transition
Lands must be our sacred mission.

* Kaleva is the symbolic hero of the West Finnic (West Somian) peoples, Kale-
vala their territory, Ilmarine (Finn. Ilmarinen) their Vulcan, and Tooni (Finn.
Tuoni) their Pluto. The "transition lands" are Ingria (Vodia) and the Carelian
Isthmus. Sampo is the magic mill of Ilmarine's making. Baba Yaga, the witch of
Russian folk-tales, symbolises the "Eastern fury" (Est. *idaviha*).

Hendrik Adamson

Radiant Girls with Flying Curls

When those radiant girls with their flying curls
Trod the green in rows on their eager toes,
When those frolic maids, thin as early blades,
With their lips of laughter and their cheeks of rose,
Moved to music thrilling over happy meadows, swept in dances
      filling earth with joyous shadows;
Ah, the whirlwind took them in a whistling tumult through the
      shining welcome of the gates of life.

When those radiant girls with their dancing curls
Left the meadow flowers for the pasture lands,
When those wanton maids, slim as April blades,
Sank in forest bowers, fell to other hands;
Ah, the pipes ceased shrilling over wilted meadows and the feet
      fled chilling earth with gloomy shadows,
And the whirlwind took them in a whistling fury, took the
      brightest blossoms of my vanished spring.

Skiff

Far skies are crackling with fuel of stars;
The sunset soughs like surf;
Dusk, putting hands to the trees' close bars,
Shakes down a blossom scurf.

Night shyly peeps in through the darkened glass,
Loose fingers pressing on lip.
The dwarf-shifts move like ants in the grass
With their water-sieves adrip.

Tangled and patterned by branch and spray,
Sickers the moon's cold light.
The beams find water-nymphs at play
In labyrinths of delight.

Along the water a shuttle-skiff glides,
Trailing a silver thread:
The night broods in its thin-ribbed sides,
And flame streaks its trenchant head.

Black heavy oars descend like flails;
The tiller veers and creaks;
Waves wag their white and friendly tails
And crease their flattering cheeks.

It is all so bewilderingly strange —
The light, the skiff, and those two
Passing there out of reach and range,
Yet heavily in view.

When the shuttle-skiff slips by house or cot
The ban-dogs howl and quake;

And some poor wretch, as like as not,
Will soon be dredged from the lake.

The hungry water smacks its lips,
Its huge maw gorged with prey.
The fatal skiff still slowly slips
Past on its sombre way.

Ah, listen how the distance rings
With laughter presaging doom!
The fading oars, like vulture wings,
Thresh the curdling gloom.

I Did Not See

Through the new-fallen gloaming ran the way,
        Traced in tobacco colour.
From among the branches, as through an open gate,
        Gleamed the new moon's horned pallor.

Walls of forest rose smoky and surface-charred
        By the slowly extinguished noons.
Dusk's long brushes had already thickly tarred
        Shrubberies anchored in floating pools.

Telegraph poles, like youths in a gawky row,
        Twitched their moustaches of wire;
Dewdrops swayed on them stickily to and fro;
        Winds sang in long-trained choir.

Mingled with winds came new and unwonted sounds
        As of tenuous singing;
Then of a sudden larger chords gladdened out
        With pinion-like swinging.

Had they struck the strings of the golden harp?
    And were they wings that came flying?
Following sand-trails, I still was strangely far
    From my wished goal and dwelling.

What is existence? What is our being?
    Heading for blind destinations,
Mourning for joy without ever seeing it,
    Preyed on by grief that is greater.

Twilight had waned, and the star-cohorts gravely
    Marched ways the sun had travelled.
Smouldering flames flashed on the darkness,
    Glinting like gold-sprinkled gravel.

I kept walking ahead through alien lands
    Past lowly walls and thatching,
And my feet foundered in the tired sand's
    Sudden and treacherous patches.

No, I did not see glitter or summer stars,
    Only a wax-faced sorrow,
And the new moon's horns pointed through wooden bars
    Towards a yet sombre to-morrow.

Delirium

Tunnelled night is rent asunder
By the hoofs of many horses,
Beating cobblestones to thunder
In their locked impetuous courses.

From the dark a fire rises;
Violent bells begin a clanging;

Tun on blood-lipped tun capsizes;
Men stack corpses fresh from hanging.

I awake out of my dreaming,
Casting off my heaviest shackles,
But I still see spilt blood streaming,
And the waiting fire crackles.

Stillness

Night is strangely still, skies as pure as day,
And the sickle moon lies upon its back.
Someone's sightless eyes grope along the way,
Anxious arms outstretched, fingers feebly bent.

Old and blind, he stalks with awakened ears,
Listening for a sound that shall lead him straight,
And he stops at once if he thinks he hears
But the timid leaf of the aspen shake.

Even shadows fear to be seen awry
And they welcome mists creeping from the cloughs.
Half-dissolved in these, see them blink awhile
Till they slowly merge with the vacant hush.

Vesperal Vision

A cloud like a giant harrow;
The moon like a cask-lid; one star
The needle of constant to-morrow;
And the sunset a bleeding furrow
Above the forest's last spar.

Beneath a fir a hut's narrow
Thin door-leaf standing ajar;
Flames gnawing birch bone and marrow;
And a voice that seems striving to borrow
Respite from griefs that shall mar.

Then a sound risen out of a burrow
And wafted from somewhere afar
Like the wail of a corpse on its barrow,
Seated swaying in lidless sorrow,
One hand on the cross's bar.

Fall and Rise

When he tossed his head cloud-high,
Water mounted to his thigh,
And for all his wary eye,
Swamp-fast he was like to die.

Wading would not bring him out;
Daylight spattered in a rout;
Sorrow claimed him bout by bout,
Filled his brain with dusk and doubt.

And he wept in shaking grief,
Then chanced on a friendly leaf,
Gathered magic in a sheaf,
And this brought him due relief.

Herbs restored his heart to day,
Set his feet upon the way,
Vivified his features' play,
Colouring what had been gray.

Armchair

Sprawled out on you in the shadows,
I am all delight and lightness.
Vividly moves my versifying,
Quicker come my quips and questions,
Truth translates, and nimble notions
Master me when your maternal
Arms enfold and gently hold me,
Muffling me in folds of twilight,
Lulling me in lush embraces,
On your soft lap's ample pillows,
On your broad upholstered bosom.

PEDRO KRUSTEN

Creator

The world went black before my vision.
A sudden storm had barred my passage,
And, throat gripped in a fierce and massive
Hate, I expected God's decision.

The world went black before my vision.
My strength ebbed, and my senses stumbled.
The evil hands drew blood that humbled
Me. I expected God's decision.

The world went black before my vision.
It seemed as if dark birds were flying
Across the heavens. There was no dying:
My last strength made its own decision.

The blood-soaked soil claimed by my power
Rose to my hands to give it fashion,
And having slain my master-passion,
I stood creator in that hour.

JUHAN SÜTISTE*

On the Camp Beach

I came to the sea verge. Green cumbrous breakers
Made hollow clamour through the day.
Gales blew in me, and landscapes faded,
And only fantasy remained.

Into this limbo a sensation
Of grief came leagued with loneliness.
Beyond them loomed a conflagration,
Limning the peaks of memory.

A timid aching grows and gathers
When all the blood is one with love:
The pulse beats fuller, feet grow feathers,
And haste would rather fly than run.

Blossomed from waves, a foam comes rolling
Beachwards to linger white and pure,
My heart sheds bitter bloom of longing,
My thoughts cling innocent to you.

* Johannes Schütz.

Dense light falls red upon the forest
Of pines. The sand glares from the beach.
One question burns in radiant torment:
Are time and we still doomed to meet?

Ah, I have carried many waters
Within, on my blood's pilgrimage,
And I have yielded to their calling,
And known the fellowship of winds.

And I would yield again, when needed,
To the long summons of the waves,
And give of life and substance freely
To walk once more love's sacred way.

I came to the sea verge. Green cumbrous breakers
Made hollow clamour through the day.
Gales blew in me, and landscapes faded,
And only fantasy remained.

Things Were No Longer as Then

Home from my travels across far-off frontiers, I burned with a
    longing,
Darling, to tell you of days bronzed by an alien sun.

But as I entered your room my delight and my pinions were
    shattered;
Things were no longer as then. Speech seemed to cleave to my
    tongue.

Ebbing a moment, your fever had left you on beaches of quiet,
And from your thin hollow cheek drained a dull current of heat.

91

Only your breathing disturbed the bound silence, and wandering
    shadows,
Flitting across your pure face, showed you indentured to
    dreams.

Long, ah! how timelessly long I stood watching you, lost and
    bewildered,
Stood till I forfeited sight, nailed to the boards at my feet.

Waking, you opened your mist-shrouded eyes, and your vision
    was timid;
And as I took your frail hand, weeping distorted your lips.

Only a week has gone by in a hopeless assertion of hoping:
Comfort has emptied its soul; work stays begun and undone.

Nor can I call up remembrance, nor pray, though I strain my
    eyes upwards,
When the sky flowers in stars, summoning silence to prayer.

Heaven is far from my will, as it always was far from our
    yearning;
God is withdrawn into calm; earth is a waste without sound;

And your mute suffering walks in my heart, waking echoes of
    horror.

Along a Wintry Highway

Slowly the frozen road rises
Out of the haugh,
Slowly the sledge with me lying
Stretched on the sawn.

Out of time's passage and bustle
Beast and man come.
Listen, the snow's very rustle
Lisps of truce won.

Shadows loom blue in the hollows,
Gaining from light;
Waiting for those that shall follow,
Banded in night.

Fluttering feet of the partridge
Trail across snow
Towards where the rimed boles are marshalled
In a steel row.

Runners shear parallel traces,
Deepening the ruts.
Tufted and cavernous spaces
Open in front.

Something of colour still tarries,
Ruddling the pines.
Clusters of crimson roan-berries
Flash their keen dye.

Wings of the gray grouse beat whirring
Into my thoughts,
Lulled till that beat by the purring
Gait of my horse.

Towards me with voice and debating
Lumbers a sledge,
Hauled by a stallion that gaily
Tosses his head.

Men's clumsy footwear are dangling
From the log tiers.
Vapours spurt, feathery and rapid,
Settling on beards.

Out of the desolate virgin
Woods nears the load,
Rankness of fir and pine clinging
Hard to the coats.

Saw's screech and sawn timber's crackling
Burst round the bend.
Furred thickets bark at the axes;
Brush and flames blend.

Where the last blizzard has drifted
Hummocks breast-high,
Pine-summits, suddenly shifting,
Fall down the sky.

Sunset's last tatters of colour
Wave to the leas.
Under white blanket and cover
Timber-piles heave.

Smoke from the bitter wood mingles
Sharply with breath.
Runners scream, harness-bells jingle,
Homing hoofs fret.

Into the whiteness of winter
March the yoked stars.
Over the stream the frost splinters
Jarring alarms.

Darkness descends on the timber;
Bridge-planking groans;
Lights and a window-pane glimmer,
Signalling home.

Homestead

When, time enlarged, you turn the corner
That brings the gray logs into view,

The cattle stare at you in warning,
The watch-dog's jaws are flecked with spume.

But, true as then, your father crosses
Towards you from the untended flats,

And through the tissues of your body
Thrills the firm greeting of his hand.

Work holds him still: his hitched-up trousers
Reveal the acid tan of peat.

His voice how honest to your mouthing!
His words how simple to your speech!

What has survived the generations
Has changed but little here with time.

Embers still tick in ash-choked places,
And boughs point leafage into light.

Too soon arrives the mood of parting;
You start with an unwilling foot

To friendly barks and children's laughter,
And saddened heart regrets: How good!

Fog

Wave and swell have flattened into lifeless glass,
And the muted sea is menacingly calm.

From the shore the globes and searchlights scarcely show;
In the sky's abysses cold sparks faintly glow.

All the air is folding into vaporous palls,
Woven of the meshes of the fog's great trawls.

From glassed sea to zenith light turns ashen gray;
Star and star are fading on the Milky Way.

Walls of desperation close round silently;
Noise of engines ceases on an agony.

Clamouring, the massive anchor-chain runs out
Into nothingness that chills the eye with doubt.

Sirens' screams are followed by a hollow boom.
Fog, gray fog! The vessel seems to jostle doom.

Ah, those sounds seem fashioned by despairing lips,
And their horror weals the sense like stinging whips.

See, a monstrous shadow looms and passes by.
Is it some lost ship, or nightmare of the eye?

Loosed from shape and motion, time and space have blent,
Leaving sight and finger neither seam nor rent.

Everywhere the brooding calm of primal spawn;
Yet a light is eating through the leaguering wall.

Motionless the waters lie in heavy murk;
Hidden worlds are waiting for another birth.

Heiti Talvik

Baptism

Flame streaked along the lightning's crackling train;
A reek of burning struck into my senses;
The tempest's stony shrilling won terrain;
And granite hail crashed through the loose defences.

A thunder-cloud, swelling like quarry smoke,
Poured out its lap in an unending torrent,
And, where the lightning-gutted heavens broke,
A shadow fell on me, winged and abhorrent.

An eagle fiercer than Medusa's dyes
Sank its twin claws into my brain's tough leather;
Green malice stared out of its frozen eyes;
And hail beat down on each triumphant feather.

It has stayed with me since — an evil shade
That urges my sick senses towards their pyre.
Already, where my dream-leaves lie decayed,
Spring the black tongues of life's deciduous fire.

Crapulence

From the discrowned tree-tops the black mists pitter;
Strong taint of plague blows where the trenched road passes;
Worms crawl out whitish from abated grasses;
And rain and spawn have made the soaked earth glitter.

How loathsome life is! Limbs in perspiration,
The drunkard eyes his birch beside a meadow.
The noose shakes in his hand. Commiseration
And autumn muffle him in bannered shadow.

Girl in April

All the spiced wines of pleasure
Flowed to my heart with vernal
Noons, but delights past measure
Made their own shadows eternal.

Tears stain the loves we cherish;
Bitterness pairs with desire.
Fold me close till I perish,
Scorched in your wings of fire.

Lord, was one ever exempted
From the contagion of malice?
Oh, how at times I am tempted
To envenom your chalice!

Treachery breeds from affection;
But when your iron is driven
Into my heart, my dejection
Pierces the seventh heaven.

Evening Song

Burning growth no longer pushes
From my wreath of solar fire.
Out of whispering trees and bushes
Step ranked shapes in black attire.

Shadows seek retreating havens,
Following the keels of colour.
Who has scattered plumes of ravens
Where the sward is growing duller?

Who has dared to flake and scour
Gold-leaf from the clouds' red masses
And to blot the patterned flower
From the canvas of the grasses?

Do not ask. The panes flush yellow,
As the folded dusk advances.
Home now! The new night is mellow
With to-morrow's even chances.

Dance of Death

Rust is gnawing at plough and harrow;
Rats crawl out of their holes in a smother;
Flame-spitting robots in trenched and narrow
Streets are preying on one another.

Everywhere lighted fuses are burning;
Things are crammed into bundle and package;
Time at its turning
Howls for wreckage.

100

Never were days less vowed to hallows:
Pavements are choked with desperate lumber;
Priestly shapes on the serried gallows
Sag in slack and staring slumber.

Jerky shadows take fright and scatter,
Seeing the drunken prophet dancing,
Perched on a powder cask that shall shatter
Bars to new worlds now advancing.

Lucifer's Song

I heard your hand upon my spirit's portal
And rushed to open this in bridal pallor.
But I have not slaved for you with each mortal
Pulse.

There has been enough in me of valour
To lacerate your pride and flout your vision,
To hurl myself down from the temple wall,
And yearning for your love in mock derision,
To perish in my fall.

Morning

Daylight slashed a glowing
Wound into my tissues,
And my blood went flowing
Out to valiant issues.

We have ceased to nourish
Visions drained of power;

Tougher growths shall flourish
In this vital hour.

Stones of law and reason
Hinder us no longer;
This is our season,
Marshalled with the stronger.

Hail the rampant charger
On night's challenged mountain!
Light's terrain grows larger
With each unsealed fountain.

Refugee

Weak, I halted by the forest's mearing,
Walking ways whose name was Who-knows-whither;
Creeping grass-haulms now disturb my hearing,
And my mouth tastes wild seed blowing hither.

Who cares here for all my recent singing?
Cannon-thunder limns the distant scene.
These cool depths are now my home, and springing
Shrubs and grasses proffer me their green.

As I drink that green and press the heather's,
I can feel my bird's heart growing feathers.

Betti Alver

Demon of Liberty

Leave resigned consent to the humble;
We are doomed to wander and stumble
In the wake of an errant light
Through the swamp's enveloping night.
Round about us the battle rages,
But you admonish me: Others' wages!
All my longings and loves seem unblessed
When your finger touches my breast.

You shall succumb to no alien power
Though you bleed and your frayed thews cower,
Though your liberty is decried.
Let the orthodox faithful deny you;
Heretic forces shall always stand by you,
And ascetics in burning pride.

Cannibal

I know that zeal is coloured with a faint
Sweetness, that lust is blent with something rotten,
That jealousy exhales an acrid taint,
And dreams a fragrance not to be forgotten.
I know that moonbeams have a quiet taste,
That sweating stone is not without its savour,
That prints, once free from touch of glue or paste,
Like fruits, have each a rich peculiar flavour.
Although experience tells me that the earth
Has edibles to suit each painted season,
My hunger now and then discovers dearth
Beyond repair of argument and reason.
My eyes shall bless oases in that land
Where waters mirror pure angelic fires,
And yet I fear that ready tooth and hand
May yield to dormant cannibal desires.

In the Jewish Quarter

Now the ghetto is shaken by violent skies,
Bringing gloom to the generations,
And the synagogue flashes angry eyes,
Like one muttering imprecations.
Other sounds are suddenly put to flight
By a shriek that seems unending.
One is reading the Talmud by candlelight;
One is getting on with his mending.
Bones are rotting in yards where rillets purl,
Scooped and fed by heavy showers.
By a window lingers a swarthy girl,
Rapt among the dusty flowers.

There she stands, marcelled and smartly dressed,
And her poppy-red lips pout unsated,
As she gazes, remote and undistressed,
At one rudely decapitated.

Not a Phantom to Work Upon

Not a phantom to work upon
The sense like a mocking spell,
But a labyrinthine hotel
Is my flowering skeleton.

These frank and these secret places!
These corridors winding to error!
The mirrors disclose strange faces;
My heart beats terror.

When lights in the rooms are extinguished
And the weary guests are sleeping,
Bent treacherous shapes come creeping,
Whose eyes cannot be distinguished.

Through multiplying fear
I feel my mouth grow arid:
If I knew where I shall be carried
When I have to go from here!

Titans

No, do not believe that even the least
Of our thoughts dissolves and forfeits its power;
In the other world, as some giant beast
Or angel, it waits for its later hour.

So passion decays, rage withers like grass,
Leaving husks in the mould that the weather bleaches:
Our bodings and dreams are but track and pass
To wanderers bound for oracular beaches.

Beyond the circled terrain of the stars
Begins the titan state's blinding splendour;
But the mind of man, scorning clogs and bars,
Has explored it and shackled its last defender.

When our world is destroyed and there is no need
For the titans to leave the refuge of heaven,
Their flaming hands shall yet fashion the seed
Of a new race tainted with death's old leaven.

My Double

May that night be accursed when, undreading the worst,
I laid up this pestilent trouble:
Taking needle and thread I assembled the head
And the ludicrous shape of my double.

Did I laugh out aloud as he strutted and bowed,
As he tumbled in spite of my warning?
He was shy as a bird and obeyed every word,
And he slept at my bedside till morning.

O the devilish sleight! He grew bold overnight,
And his laughter declared him my master.
Blood grew cold in my veins, and my griefs were his gains,
And I stared in the eyes of disaster.

Now he leers at my plight both by day and by night,
And I fly from his wit's stabbing flashes.
See, my hair has gone gray and my body agley,
And my sight has been silted with ashes.

Black Madonna

When I see pictures of her sacred figure,
My mind recalls a woman ringed with sands
And rocks, and on the smooth and swarthy vigour
Of that broad bosom four caressing hands.
Of her two children one, his eyes reflecting
The light's unfathomed immemorial springs,
Sees the bold columned corridors connecting
The worlds like a design of branching wings.
The other child, drawn by uncurbed desire
Towards the unending night of an abyss,
Dreams with his rapt and sentenced eyes on fire,
As if poised on that fatal precipice.
O Black Madonna, I too am a mother
With two small children drawing equal breath:
I tread the peaks with one, and with the other
Am doomed at last to fall to my long death.

Bread

Where the dusk blows heavier weather,
Shapes break vaguely from the heather,
Cheekbones wet and with hobbled foot.
Stubble-field and kiln-house boarding,
Cabin-bench and handy hoarding
Blacken with denser human soot.

107

These are wills assigned to gleaning.
Through long days and barred unmeaning
Nights the mind bleeds from its gashes,
Last light perishes on lashes,
And the sweat splays salty fingers.
At the doorpost anguish lingers,
Piping in a doomed to-morrow,
Grief, and sorrow.

How the active beaches shimmer!
But where care makes dimness dimmer
Can the bones and sinews win?
Storms hoist straw-sails out of stubble,
Spatter out the pain and trouble
Battened in the ordered bin.

Gales and hail make sudden clatter.
Only stumps remain to shatter
Huddled hopes in heaps of barley.
Ripe ears burst against the gnarly
Bark, and corn spurts out to moulder
On a boulder.

Bind the precious grain in sacking.
But the whirlwinds take what's lacking,
Twist and tangle up the cords.
In the scatter-witted raking
Mill Time's kith and kin are shaking
Loose the knots behind the boards.

There are notches in the reaping
Hook, and weary lightnings, leaping
Rarer, light the long dream's edges.
But your harvest is not ended.

Reap with bended
Back till bins redeem your pledges.

Not a speck of lustre shivers
Through the bleak and vacant view,
But the polecat's anger quivers,
Stretching claws to reach at you.
And the day is drab and leaky.
With a burden on your creaky
Back, you mill in clay-bound station,
Waiting death's illumination.
Past your knowing,
This. Keep going,
Charged to save yourself as granger
From raw danger.

But your going is impeded;
Bread poods, mildewed, lie unheeded,
Cannot rise above disaster.
Toil on, beaded
Sweat. You're master!

Flames come hissing from the stack;
Columned smoke maps out the track.
Corn-beads moisten. Hurry, hurry!
You may weep your tears of worry
As a dew for shoot or petal,
But your hands shall pour the grain
On to metal,
Crimson with a fiery pain.

Vapours mount, the furnace blazes;
Life-sap fevers in the hazes;
Ears and temples fill with purring;
Blood strikes lightnings from the broiling

Eyeballs. Keep the grain-heaps stirring,
Safe from spoiling,
Safe from ailing
Under strength grown unavailing.

Heavily you start your crawling,
Groping for the dipper, gripping
Edges, falling,
Weak and dripping.
Now the souls of nightmare dreaming,
All the real and the seeming
Knead and mingle into one.
Loved and loving vision scorches
In the heat of flaring torches
Into ghosts of dead and done.
Red rings clamp into the ceiling;
Furnace jaws disgorge black reeling
Smoke, voluminous and gritty.
Pity! Pity!

See, the soot's grimed finger stipples
Sight. Then silver freshness ripples
In across the sill. Start making
Tracks towards the waiting grange,
But first sift the heavier taking
From the stubborn and the strange.
Shift the light sieves to the trestle;
Do not wrestle
Doubt. The gain that you've been giving
Will suffice for loaves and living.

And you set your lightened burden —
Grind-won guerdon —
By the hinges of the door.

Fear-bells cavil, blunt and brittle,
On the aspen-twigs: How little
Are the helpings of your store!

Corn-grains hiss into the timber
Bin. The heap swells smooth and limber.
Why this hurry?
Sacks grow lightish
With the flurry,
And you shovel all the whitish
Wheat into the wide container,
Thrust it in with hands, like treasure.
Now the tun is full, the strainer,
Hole and crevice, stoop and measure.

Out of doors dawn's furrow tosses
Radiance up. A pure smile crosses
Eyes and face grown still and steady.
Are you ready?
Other hands shall weigh your reaping.
Leave your sickle in the keeping
Of a beam beneath the eaves,
And with death-boards on your shoulder,
Go down, dark to chance beholder,
Deeper than the source of leaves.

There are broad garths under grasses,
Muffled rooms where no light passes.
There you lie now, nerves unshaken.
Cocks don't waken
You with crowing.
Marvellously light airs, blowing
Out of Time's tall loft, assemble
Chaff upon your lids that tremble

Now no longer where you're lying,
Done with dying.

Father Earth sifts sand and, stopping,
Listens to the slow rains dropping,
Mutters to himself, and sighs.
Harp attuned to tribulation,
Black Fall, numb to Spring's elation,
Murmur quiet lullabies.

Tailor Care

Through the slanted shower,
Past the falling shades,
Care's hand knocked at our
Door with scissor-blades

Care sewed shirts of sadness
For each eager neck,
Marred the girdle's gladness
With black streak and fleck.

And he barred the rosy
Cheeks with mourning bands,
Matched hair not with posy,
But with long white strands.

Song about a Son

Sunlight streamed, the dewdrops sparkled,
And the rain fell merrily
As the little mite was playing
White-frocked at his mother's knee.

Soon those bold young legs had measured
Paths to the marsh beyond the rye.
Tailors came and made him buttoned
Clothes with buttonholes navel-high.

Was it the wolf, that sinister haunter
Of the thickets, who howled so loud?
Our young man rode out to the forest
In his greatcoat, brave and proud.

Death ran riot; flames rose higher;
And the field of battle bled.
Son of man, you too have fallen
With the dying and the dead.

Mother was left with empty corners,
Father to groom the horse and to tote;
And the son lay in the chapel
In his wooden overcoat.

UKU MASING

One Beautiful Day

Your feet are calm to-day and do not tire
Me, but my crude eyes cannot see the hollow
Skiff of the sky where the cloud-fishes wallow
Between your passing toes in livid gyres.
My rafters blossomed out of building fires
What death-tick beetle's patient greed could swallow?
He too, released from masquerades to follow,
Lifts wings Your joy has tutored to aspire.

You, Lord, alone can call the tempest's hoary
Hands from the happy woods left in my keeping,
And spread the coming days in ordered story,
Like a green carpet blessed by prayer and sweeping
To the year's end; for, when the sun's last glory
Fails, Yours will be the only life that knows no sleeping.

August Night Ecstasy

Oh, now my complaint is ended
Against those who merit the edge of my hostile volition
And yet have not felt it.
God's empire is not more splendid,
Or the White Ship's* triumphant apparition,
For there is a moon, and a cloud-fashioned eagle,
And its straining head is I;
For there is a wind, and legend-shaken trees,
And a temple chant that is I.
That which now passes over house-tops
With the gentle tread of an elf,
That which now twitters in the verdure
Is not aware of self.
Is it not, ah joy! my heart's, my very heart's bird?

Lord God, I again feel your pure presence
Like the white wings of delight,
And to your gown clings radiance
As of virid stars in the night.
Are you not looking now through the tangled branches?
Stroking the reddening apples?
Will it ever come, if this is not the happy
Noon of my day?

O miracle! I do not regret the ruined time that blanches
Cheeks when you rise on my way,
Smiling at me through gladness,

---

* A symbol of salvation used in the prophecies of the Estonian sectarian preacher
Maltsvet. The tragic story of the vigils for the mysterious vessel is familiar to
readers of English from "The White Ship" (Finn. *Valkea laiva*) of the Finnish
authoress Aino Kallas. A fuller account will be found in Eduard Wilde's Estonian
novel *Prohvet Maltsvet*.

As if you had long expected to have word
Of me and thought: What is that sadness
Which keeps him from imagining himself to be a bird,
Shaking a white foam of pinions,
Shot with flames of sylvan green,
Envied by the sea's cloud-minions
And by those who worship the seen?
Risen flame of Manala* beaches, I am a believer
Once more, for there is a hurrying moon and a cloud-bird,
And its lost importunate head is I;
For there is a wind, and in your garden the tall trees
Are down, and there, hands raised, am I.

Song of Soldiers Retreating before Ghosts

We are trumpeters stripped of our holdings that once taught our
folly to brag,
And all that we have now are visions and each man the sorriest
nag.
The azure horizons still summon down hummocked and dust-
smothered ways,
And, if the land suddenly ceased, we should tread on a watery
blaze.
We ride on our shadows, deploying no flags but our suppliant
hands,
And we seek for the mountains of God and beyond them the
sea-washed sands.
Our horses are weary with movement, and rib bone thrusts out
beside bone;
Our swords are corroded with rust and as heavy and awkward
as stone;

* The Estonian pagan underworld, or realm of Mana, god of the dead. Toonela
(Finn. Tuonela) is a synonym. See *Kalevipoeg* and the Finnish *Kalevala*.

Our feet are naked and bleeding; our bodies are bitter with pain;
Our minds are as earth grown sodden with blood of the van-
    quished slain;
Our trumpets are dinted and broken; our anthems encumbered
    with dust;
Yet we go our predestined way, and our music pierces through
    rust.
The forests are blazing behind us, the fields full of acrid breath:
We know that our forces are followed by those of the ghost king
    Death
And that we are the last defenders, forlorn hope's ragged array,
Defeated and long abandoned, the men with arrears of pay.
Our flagging ardour is kindled by splendour of angels' wings,
But you are beyond our possession, O God of created things.
We dream of the White Ship's canvas, the trail behind us in
    flames,
And the smouldering ashes growing in heaps of forgotten names.
Our only comrade the road, we rejoice in the promised beach,
Although we know that its curve is for ever out of our reach.
It does not matter one jot where we die, for blood is to spend,
And valour that laughs at the victor was ever the dying man's
    friend.
What of it that weariness wastes us and suns beat fierce on our
    brows!
Our hearts are as light as the blossom on God's everlasting boughs.
We are trumpeters stripped of our holdings and free from the
    lead of the past;
We still have the azure horizon; our hopes are the White Ship's
    mast;
The clouds stream like pennants and signal the goal towards
    which we press;
And our eyes refigure the vision of heaven in the wilderness.

Of Nothing but Faith

Jesus, silver-eyed and robed in all your graces,
When you walked the desert, fingers gently grasping
Irised whorls and circles, not the angel faces,
Nor God's self could recognise these loathly regions.
And how soft your passage over lakes where legions
Of fish fry moved freely! But your hand felt grasses,
Where a tiny fish the storms had tossed lay gasping
In its final throes, blind to the light that passes.
And you picked it up and walked on slowly, seeking
For its kin from which but violent storms could sever
It. Then these once found, its new love started speaking:
"Saviour, I would stay with you from now for ever."

Jesus, I repeat your name like kind caresses
To the dusk, the lamplight, and the lights fixed higher.
Do you know, the echo of your footfall blesses?
Wanderer in wastes, I bow to you with laughter
And I gladly clasp my hands in dust-stained prayer.
Cull me candid heavenly lilies that hereafter
These may grace the Dead Sea's topmost lifeless layer.
There is not a joy to equal that of singing
How you walk the coloured world in shine and shower,
Or of kneeling where your feet have taught the clinging
Earth and buried bones to put out leaf and flower,
Or of loving you as stars are loved by one in prison —
Brilliant stars, and trees, and the white-winged and airy
Drift of summer clouds. Ah, when you had arisen,
Was the earth still mute to the brown feet of Mary?

Only the Mists Are Real

Winds are whirled spindles that use has not worn;
I but a tenuous tissue of gloom
That God's taper fingers of one-piece bone
Wove in the stars' warm weaving-room.
Winds are whirled spindles. But who has said
What is the yarn of the earth's faced shrouds?
Frail lustre of mists, say, their essence fled,
Spent that my head did not reach to the clouds.

Easter Credo

Sixty-eight are the fiery wheel's revolutions,
These and perhaps no more,
Then come the funeral of azure flowers and cloudy ablutions,
And the cross lies at heart's door.
Add for your friend a few days culled from ample heaven,
Dusty with vernal leaves;
Plant in your body a tree that has shaded the level
Of his eyes' pendent eaves.
Ere the pure stars are extinguished and light enlarges,
See my mounting path swing;
Ere the shepherds have piped together their charges
I have come on a cooling spring.
I am sure that as heaven's azure plies doming,
As Rā is the name I was given at birth,
I shall live on the day of my golden body's homing,
Bone-blossoms springing from earth.

HILDA ESKO*

Haunted Nights

The spectral hour of midnight is at hand,
And my hot aching lids are still unable
To feel the cool forgetfulness of sand,

But watch the past's wan corpse upon the table.
My eyes are dull with agonising pain
No power can extinguish or disable.

Like the slow heavy drops of autumn rain,
The rain of minutes settles down to falling,
And each big drop spells terror to my brain.

The hangman fits his noose, and the appalling
Dark brings together by what devious ways
The ruck of memories and the constant calling

Voices that grope through the nocturnal maze,
The sudden fits of horror-stricken weeping,
The curses disembodied by the haze,

* Hilda Saks.

120

Mingling with vicious bayonets and the creeping
Dawn mists. My dark brain's spindles spin
An endless chain of memories that, leaping

And falling, claim my eyes. I see the whin,
The glint of misty puddles as I wander
Across a marsh amid the screeching din

Of shells, and I have even time to ponder
On what shall be my fate — the fusillade,
Last fear of refugees with fears to squander.

Enough! My desperation must have prayed
That some protecting trench or hole should blind me
To all the things of which I was afraid

And only the compassionate moonlight find me.
But here to-night, in league with sleeplessness,
Those unrelenting memories still bind me.

And once again I live through dead distress:
I see the vicious play of conflagration,
In which, through sanguinary storm and stress,

Burning roofs fall in grim reiteration,
And then the final furious dances start
On that green sward which witnessed youth's elation.

A new and sudden horror grips my heart:
A trapped beast roars out as the rampant yellow
Flames lick the byre with tongues that crawl and dart.

I see a rush, then panic, and that fellow
Fall as a monster with a burning wall
Upon its back tramples him with a bellow.

Its great hoofs kindled in the blazing stall,
The maddened bull careers about and tosses
An onlooker as lightly as a ball.

A ball? Ah, no! It is the moon that crosses
The window, scattering its tinsel light
And singling out the objects for its glosses.

May the benignant lustre of the night
Temper my tortured senses with its blessing
When the last parting moment comes in sight.

And when that moment comes all these distressing
Sights shall be blotted out. Only a tale,
Remote and passionless, shall live confessing

Dead griefs. For us oblivion shall prevail.

Bernard Kangro

Vernalia

The warm spring draws new blades from last year's tussocks
And over boughs and branches spreads a greenish
Film. The gay rye-braird scuttles with the breezes,
And buttercups proclaim approaching summer.
The birch-trees perched upon a drying hummock
Suspend over my head their furtive fleeces,
And the black alders have renewed their leases,
Paying the spring with darkening berry-clusters.

Over the haugh the curlew broadly sketches
Its shape on bird-limed kexes as it passes
In heavy flight. The wind-swept face of heaven
Is clouding with the rain's lank hair that stretches
Towards the warm zenith. And the blackbird leavens
All this with songs that stitch me to the grasses.

Woman of the Fens

From the gray circle of the fen-pine's matted
Roots the fen swims into a reeded lake,
Where shallows glisten from among the stakes
Of bulrushes and dark pools lie at anchor.
Coming down from the steep and shadowed hanger,
We glimpsed the fresh hope of a virid vein
That pointed towards a tract of brushwood plain
And led us over soft unstable landscape.

The damp soil steamed. Misled by lichened rootlets,
Her leg slid deep into the greedy fen,
And her skirt's hem, grown sopping, snared me. Then,
As she went down before my pent-up passion,
My raw mouth bled under the tumbled cushion
Of dwarf shrubs from the werwolf's fangs and fury.

Happy Blades of Grass

You had spent days on end in damping hazes
When suddenly the sun unsealed the beaches
To light, and the obscure despondent mazes
Of your heart's journey straightened to clear reaches.

The sun sets now in a quite different fashion
And rises different, the forlorn stars banished.
The cage that once enclosed you and your passion,
Like netted birds, has altogether vanished.

And yet you do not dare to leave these places
For fear of drowning in the sun's abiding

124

Radiance. Grass springs already in your traces,
And tiny buds of hope are there in hiding.

Do you not dread their loveliness that lingers,
Or the insidious scent of poisonous flowers?
Ah no! You pick them with untiring fingers
To lay them out in rows through drying hours.

Dew breeds its cloud, and this, like all clouds, passes,
And your inordinate love will surely tire
Of spring, yet blade-like from among the grasses,
Years lapsed, you may arise in virid fire.

Old Houses

Let us demolish these houses,
Strip them of rafters and beams,
Open up flues where heat drowses,
Silence the tucked-away crickets,
Singing their songs full of dreams.

Axes, resound on the ceiling;
Loosen the stones, iron bar;
Grip fast, tongs, unsealing
Doors and gates and wickets;
Teeth of the long saw, scar,

Leaving raw jagged edges.
Now the destruction is done,
And from its stony ledges,
See, the mullein lifts yellow
Malice into the sun,

Wheeled to its setting and mellow.

Drowning

The sun's striations glitter like fishes' eyes and scales.
This denser world is bitter and sealed to travellers' tales.

Water is slowly clotting like ale upon my face,
And subtle mists have blotted the charms of time and place.

My hair sinks roots in mire as soon as I touch ground;
The greedy lid has started to stop my ears to sound.

While I lie here a broken and useless thing of clay,
Somewhere faint chimes betoken a crowded wedding-day,

And somewhere too a brindled cat frets in throes of lust,
And over all the kindled sun glares through settling dust.

Forest

Every winter the hare would come to our garth
To repair the season's losses,
And squirrels would scuttle on log and thatch,
And the goat champ the wall's gray mosses.

A troop of partridge would rise in flight
From the barn with a sound of snapping;
The banded magpie would drop at our door,
And the woodpecker keep on tapping.

As tame as a kitten and eager for milk,
A hedgehog would slip from the tillage;
And one black and sinister autumn night
The wolf came to slaughter and pillage.

The covetous aspen had reached our gate,
And lindens the garden fences;
Red ants crawled in thousands all over the walls;
And the death-tick pierced our defences.

The death-tick kept ticking the doom of our croft
Till at length its days were counted:
The rustling forest invaded our garth,
And leaves sprang where smoke had mounted.

Deathmath

Shadow-curves are drawn across the autumn-tinted stubble,
And the scythe-like norther sweeps across the earthy rubble.

I have driven stakes to hold the meadow loam's last foison
And have wept my blood into a slow corrosive poison.

I have gathered up at length the dried swath of my mowing
And have spread it under floors where no stray winds come
     blowing.

Full of hopeless thoughts, I sit here now beside the fire:
Where shall I put hands upon strong cattle for the byre?

What will pull and champ the early grasses of the meadows?
Only herds of death that move as silently as shadows?

Here I sit alone and watch the light and darkness mingle,
And I suddenly make out strange creatures round the ingle.

I am haunted: see, the creatures multiply like berries.
Death's dun cattle stand about me, sinister and serried.

127

Timeless Memory

As I win the kiln to fancy,
I assume its scope and station.

Over me the grain-bars cluster,
And within my ribs there rages
An imperious conflagration.
Perched on bars in serried muster,
Sheaves emit an acrid vapour.
Men as mum and black as kobolds,
Handling sheaf-rods and by rote,
Pass across the kiln's red throat.

And when firelight takes them fairly,
All those faces seem familiar:
Here they chored who knows how early
Through time's flux and hurly-burly;
Here they lived and toiled and moved.

These my forbears, now my neighbours,
Fill the kiln-room of the ages,
Strong, untiring in their labours,
Shadowy on the blazing light.

I, the kiln in scope and station,
Feel how in my bones there rages
A compelling conflagration
Through the long unwearied night.

Late Home-Coming

Skies are flooded from the core
Of the dark. A bleak wind moans.

Through the snow, behind you, trailing
Wolf-packs follow.
Feverishly you try each door;
Every nerve inside you groans;
Narrow moonlight, crossed and failing,
Inks each hollow.

Night shapes day, and day shapes night;
Nearly all the stars are blind;
Misty veils, unfurled and dripping,
Smother heaven.
Take that turning to the right;
Close the guardian gate behind;
Don't let go the axe, keep gripping,
Strong as seven.

What new sound is that you hear?
Surely tramp of others' feet.
Have you reached the house already
By some wonder?
But the hearth is cold and drear,
And the oil-lamps give no heat.
Back! The kiln-room, wide and ready,
Hides its thunder.

Challenge

To-night there is heavier breathing
As the tempest wrenches at latches;
The leaf-stripped birches are seething;
The gales tear at tousled thatches.

Night and day have lost their succession;
Skies snap in streaming sorrow;

But my mind is still in possession
Of light and to-morrow.

The chimney-flue howls as if hounded
By the wild gloom's harrying tides,
And here am I, pinned and surrounded
By hatred in werwolves' hides.

Come, let us match fangs in battle,
Rabid brutes from the heather;
I am armed now, although I grazed cattle
And sheep in fine weather.

Swamps of War

Forest trails. The gray marsh lichen.
Pools of water everywhere.
Melancholy crane-throats calling
Over there.

Cart-ruts deepen. Do not linger!
Mud shows up a horse-shoe track.
Here, close by, fresh graves yawn, densely
Filled with black.

Within earshot muffled striding
Of the war-boot into night.
Veiled in smoke and cloud-beleaguered,
Fades last light.

Iron-Bringer

Iron-bringer from the marches,
Rise from fen and stagnant pool.
Take up fistfuls of the rusty
Iron's being.
Dyes of heaven's dissolving arches,
Spill blood, fleeing.
Strike deep, trusty
Iron, born in unnamed places.

We have drunk, know foreign faces,
Lost what noble words were spoken.
But the iron keeps its power,
Bedded in the fen's moist night.
Weeds have woven close unbroken
Webs to ward off sight and day.
Wait for the relieving light,
And your beam shall point the way.

See, the iron-bringer rises,
And his hill bursts into flame.
Ready eye assays the prizes,
Ready arm the rust-bred power.
Light, which matched the dying hour,
Springs anew in dye and name.

Old Vôrumaa*

Whoever hoards his pittance miser-fashion
Shall never see the riches he has lost.

* One of the south-eastern provinces of Estonia.

A kindlier fate shall spare my greater passion
And give me back my love's excelling cost.

Once a sweet muse, known to another nation,
Blessed the old exile sold to slavery.
Now Sunday's child shall suffer transformation:
The muse's loving touch shall kindle me.

I will arise, and my beleaguered senses
Shall find release from agonies and years.
I will return as the new light condenses,
Buoyed up by faith unshaken by my tears.

For there is not a hand that shall deprive
Me, Vôrumaa, of you who are alive.

K ARL RISTIKIVI

Hårsfjärden

> *Sing me a song of a lad that is gone.*
> *Say, could that lad be I?*

Once I was young and Arcadia-bound,
Though I was born in a hovel.
Sometimes I muse with my feet on the ground:
Oh, to be young and Arcadia-bound,
Safe from the pick and the shovel!

But like so many another I've lost
Track of the signs to those bowers,
And to discover them now it would cost
More than the dreams of the youth that I've lost,
More than my physical powers.

Where shall I go then? The water is there,
Lined with cold rocks and dead beaches,
And the last boatman has left with his fare,
Singing to warn me the water is there,
Singing of channels and reaches.

So here I am, and I really don't know
Where I shall waken to-morrow.
Don't try to tell me it's good to be so;
Life, after all, is like that. You don't know
The depth of an exile's sorrow.

KERSTI MERILAAS

Once I Shall Yield Myself Up for Ever

Once I shall yield myself up for ever:
My heart will be changed to earth and buried,
And my soul will journey along the wind's river
To the moon under tents of cloudy hurry.

And I shall be free from myself completely,
Free from the prickings of sense and desire:
I shall fall by the wayside as dust, or a fleeting
Sunbeam, or ash from a windy gyre.

And at the golden approach of summer
I shall open buttercup-eyes at the parting
Of ways and see the azure and comely
June days come and sit at my side on the grasses.

I shall hold the blackbird's tiny bower
In the poplar's resin-scented hollow
Hand and one morning break out in flower —
In yellow-green camomile over the fallows.

When the grain is hard and white and the setting
Sun tells the ageless autumn fable
Of the crops, I shall be the earth's sweet blessing —
A morsel of bread on the labourer's table.

Evening on the Beach

Evening followed the sea's failing riot,
Coming up with faint fish odours.
Soft white mists had gradually risen
In a close-meshed flight out of their prison
In the reeds, promising rest and quiet.

High above, the sky's steel arches rigid
Over pallid soughing water.
Solemnly, one following the other,
Stone steps after stone into the smother
Of the sea, back bent and humbly frigid.

Ah, the burdened day was hard to carry:
One word said across his shoulder
Stayed my dreams in their momentous thronging,
But my heart is still obsessed with longing
To surrender, though his ardour tarry.

Here I write his name on wet expanses
In a kind of desperation,
Till my longing ultimately tires,
And I seek the kindling of new fires
In the ash of losses and foiled chances.

Angry Autumn

The wind loosens leafage
From branches and bushes,
And water-bred vapours sprout
Up from the rushes.

The rain-swollen torrent
Bites into both hollow
Brown banks, and the turnings
Tempt its fury to follow.

Shrubs stand by the roadside
Like tumbledown byres,
And here and there maple-leaves
Jet angry fires.

Cloud piles upon cloud-bank
In layers of copper,
And bronze drizzles earthward
As out of a hopper.

Then all unexpected
Strange shadows assemble:
Your hands lift, beseeching,
Your lost limbs tremble.

Saint

Struck into a mountain, one black cross
Speaks the martyrdom of your last hour,
And the pilgrim mourns the ancient loss,
Proffering his sorrow in a flower.

Here, where the foul plague once rioted,
Dying lips invoked your name and glory,
And steps only later steps have hid
Came in awe to learn your healing story.

Holy water seethed in font and bowl,
And the temple veil rent to derision,
But before your comprehending soul
Passed the sacred rood's triumphant vision.

Ah, your soul is out of reach of those
Who have sought your robes and dead belongings.
You are like a child whose dreaming knows
Even raindrops harbour deathless longings.

Seas subside and cleave at your approach,
And the foam spreads out in calm surrender.
Round about your path the ranks encroach,
Marshalled in the grace of angel splendour.

Slaughter Day

When the mists curl up from the water
And the cock crows the daylight back,
Once again the Michaelmas slaughter
Starts by the ominous timber-stack.

From the pen comes a sound of chewing
As the bar is raised from the door.
He is here with his sack, renewing
Spattered suns of the years before.

Sure hands part the young from their mothers,
Holding cabbage-leaves out as bait,

Till at length from among the others
Trots the children's love and mate.

There she goes unaware of error,
Small hoofs cracking the brittle ice,
When of a sudden a naked terror
Grips her bowels as in a vice.

How she struggles, her eyeballs staring
At the blade worn strangely thin!
Where the new day's torch lifts flaring
Droops a cloud like a blood-stained skin.

AUGUST SANG

It Was Autumn

It was autumn. Light stood mellow
In the quiet places.
Down slow littered walks the yellow
Leaves lisped summer's graces.

Was the air not doomed to harden,
Tall suns firmly banished?
Hazes ravelled park and garden,
Shapes grew bent and vanished.

Red still flowed through open shutters
Over skyline meadows;
Then this failed, and only mutters
Shredded through the shadows.

Nocturnalia

Choking a cry of terror, I emerge
Out of a dream and see fixed eyes and hollow

Chaps fade into the dusk. An alien urge
Summons me into sentience, and I follow.

I rise and leave the house. Cloud fingers graze
The livid moon. I hear the distance sighing
And hasten through the rain-swept murk down ways
That lead to slopes where serried trees are plying.

The gales howl, waters seethe and churn, the reeds
Rustle. A lighthouse is the only token
Of life. Out of the night's abyss white steeds
Come charging towards the beach to fall there broken.

The sky is rent, and a long radiance falls
In an immense and stationary shower
On waters black as blood. My God! These squalls,
This rain, this darkness, how I love their power!

Walls

By the time life's rounding kernel
Had begun to change its flavour,
Youth's light passed that seemed eternal,
And the later light grew graver.
Here you sit, high and forsaken,
Meditating care and joy,
Turning over what was taken
From you to the puniest toy.

Once you breathed a cleaner air,
Faced the windy sun's bright sallies;
Now you are condemned to stare
At the cobblestones in alleys;
And the sunlight falls in patches,

141

Or the windows stream with rain.
Thus it went these weeks in snatches;
Thus it goes and will again.

Narrow stair and cell-niched warren,
Where the yellow inmate lingers —
Here you move along the barren
Passages with groping fingers,
And your forces fail and languish
Like the lives sapped here before,
And the whitewashed walls sweat anguish,
And fear locks each silent door.

Golgotha

Fires fail in the troubled weather
That springs from the waters below,
And feather by wet feather
Falls the late autumn snow.
The mood is bent towards sorrow
And weighing of thoughts that dull
On this night as far from to-morrow
As the cry of that desolate gull.

The hill looms in night's possession
As a radiance creases the sky;
Armed men come in close procession
With torches lifted high.
Are you in the force that presses
Up the hill? Is the rood for you?
And are yours the sharp distresses
Vacant eyes have come to view?

142

The soldiers make a beginning;
Salvation grows bile at the mouth;
The symbol of sinner and sinning
Affronts the gale from the south.
Rain patters on helmet metal;
The god is nailed to the rood;
The eyes disperse; griefs settle
On loyal vigil and mood.

Your footfall flags through the sighing
Of the barren autumn winds;
Your thoughts are strained on dying,
With the thoughts of defeated minds.
Rain courses down helmet metal;
God hangs from the ominous rood;
And suns in their millions settle
On nights in the Golgotha mood.

Expectant

Night and cold brought restless slumber;
Tissues of gray dewfall bound me.
Now I wake to touch and tremor,
And the light is warm around me.

Perfume of exotic spikenard
Lifts me from the earthly level.
In her voice moves silver gladness,
In her glance a golden revel.

And I lay my aching burden
Down before flamboyant fountains,
And my burning on the pyre
Is like song ascending mountains.

143

KALJU LEPIK

By the Waters of Toonela *

Faint distant stars are shining,
And the night wind blows rank.
Here am I stalking the death-bird
On this dead bank.

Tipped in a Karjala† smithy,
This is the shaft I have chosen,
Knowing the bird of death
Waits for death from my bowstring.

Now in their final flight,
See how the great wings quiver.
God! I am borne into night,
Borne down the darkened river.

* The Estonian Hades, or abode of death, known also as Manala.
† Carelia.

Wooden Crosses

At thickets of wooden crosses
The moon's bloodless snout
Barks out its aching lustre.

Helmets with noiseless mouths
Open in frozen laughter.

Tempests of February
Strive with the brass of words
Over heroic blood fallen.

Snowdrifts smother each laugh
In thickets of wooden crosses,
Meaningless wooden crosses.

Kalju Ahven

Shadows

Shadows in endless procession come slowly and solemnly past,
Dim, and with hair flying loose, or with battle-scarred head
     bandaged fast.

Silent, they march in the silence, their footfalls as hushed
     as the night,
Joy on their faces, for is not the end of their journey in sight?

Over their eyes the white bandages darken from wounds that
     still bleed.
Death was so valiant and proud, for they fought that their land
     should be freed.

Thousands of faces pass by me. My friends and my brother
     are there.
Shame fills my heart as I stand, and that shame is akin to
     despair.

Their way was open to all who would choose — it was open to me.
I chose another alas! and that way has led over the sea.

Now in magnificent silence that endless procession goes past.
Shadows, dim shadows, they pass me; but see, I am with them
      at last.

ARVED VIIRLAID

I Waken

I waken.
My heart is filled with wonder;
I have had a vision
Of your sweet and smiling beauty.

I waken.
Light in triumph
      greets me to-day,
Flower-bells are ringing
      outside my wide-open window,
And streamlets' arpeggios
      come with gracious woodland songs.

I waken.
Your laughter sparkles
      in the blue glance of heaven;
Your hands are in breezes
      that caress the billowing cornfields;
And your fragrance
      reaches me through every flower.

And your whisper
        is like a golden fairy-tale
        in a sultry haystack.

I waken
        and become as song.
The skylark's swift reverberant shuttles
Fashion me
        into a shimmering fabric.
Such things make the day
Above the fields and the lakes and the woodlands
        a shining
                graciousness.

Ah, you are everywhere beside me,
Although
You are in our far-off homeland
Fast asleep
In the birch's shadow
Under a blanket of white flowers.

Ivar Grünthal

Liberators

Their work completed with the fallen night,
The righteous hundred-headed troop can snore.
A sizzling spit proclaims the latest score —
A lamb flayed by those shadows on the light.
Horse-hoofs have churned the road up to the right;
The air absorbs the corpse-stench more and more;
The skyline spurts up aching blood galore
That mingles red with russet, life with blight.

No crowing cock shall greet a sight to harrow,
For bird, like man, was not conceived in grace.
A girl hangs from the well-beam, limp and narrow,
The violator's filth across her face.
The plundered cottage is no more a haven
To life, save to the goggling long-beaked raven.

RAIMOND KOLK

Mad Dog

In he came and, safe from weather,
Slumped against the bedpost scowling.

Rain and wind beat down together;
Packs of maddened dogs were howling;

Darkness stripped white fangs that, flashing,
Snarled in restive expectation;

Tongues hung out between the gnashing
Fangs to jeer at his frustration.

In he came into the cabin,
Came and rolled his lost eyes inwards.

REET VEER*

I Will Come

I will come if even the virgin wood
On your loam lies scattered like skittles,
If flints are heaped where the soil was good,
And the stranger's knife still whittles.

I will come as soil to your barren stones;
My blood shall be spring and shower;
The saw shall raze the wood of my bones,
And fields suck strength from its dower.

My thoughts shall breed beasts and birds in trees,
My soul be the rib to creation.
And work shall revive, and song ride the breeze,
And the sun recreate his elation.

You shall live through me and blossom anew,
Be exempt from despair and aggression,
Till the day when the flints reappear to view
Beneath my initial transgression.

* Reet Vellner.

INDEX OF AUTHORS

INDEX OF ORIGINAL TITLES WITH SOURCES

INDEX OF ORIGINAL TITLES WITH SOURCES

ANTHOLOGY OF MODERN ESTONIAN POETRY

ARTUR ADSON:

HENRIK VISNAPUU:

HENDRIK ADAMSON:

INDEX OF ORIGINAL TITLES WITH SOURCES